THE DEEP-FRYER COOKBOOK

THE DEEP-FRYER COOKBOOK

WENDY SWEETSER

APPLE

A QUINTET BOOK

Published by Apple Press
Sheridan House
112-116A Western Road
Hove
East Sussex
BN3 1DD

ISBN: 1 84092 457 8

This book was designed and produced by
Quintet Publishing Limited
6 Blundell Street
London N7 9BH

Project editor: Catherine Osborne
Art director: Roland Codd
Designer: Rod Teasdale
Photographer: Phillip Wilkins
Food stylist: Wendy Sweetser

Creative director: Richard Dewing
Publisher: Oliver Salzmann

Manufactured by Provision, Singapore
Printed by SNP Leefung Printers Limited, China

Contents

Introduction

ABOVE Tempura prawns with barbecue sauce.

There is no escaping the fact that if we want comfort food or a quick, satisfying snack we're probably talking 'deep-fried'.

Chips, doughnuts, fried chicken and fritters – we love them all – but can't ignore that little voice nagging away inside telling us they're nice but oh! so very, very naughty.

With many of us preoccupied these days with cholesterol, calorie counting and keeping slim, deep-fried food has attracted a bad press and literally been consigned to the back burner as steaming, dry roasting and grilling have taken over. Delicious though food cooked by these methods is, it's an inescapable fact that old habits die-hard and, for most of us, our cravings for battered fish, crisp-crumbed mushrooms or thick crunchy chips don't go away.

But is deep-fried food really so bad for us? The good news is 'no' as long as it forms part of a balanced diet. Starvation rations or completely cutting out certain groups of foods may achieve dramatic results in the short term but by depriving yourself of the foods you enjoy can make you crave them all the more, and once you fall off the wagon getting back on will become harder every time. Much better to continue eating the things you enjoy, but in moderation, so you don't end up feeling deprived.

Whilst nobody can claim that deep-fried food is low cal and suitable for every meal, it can nevertheless form part of a sensible eating plan, as long as the cook follows a few simple rules. Words like 'fatty', 'heavy' and 'soggy' might have given deep-frying a bad name but by making sure you heat oil to the correct temperature, you give food a protective coating and drain it well before serving, the adjectives shift to 'light', 'crisp' and 'delicious'. If deep-fried correctly, food should absorb no more than a couple of tablespoons per pint of oil – roughly the same as shallow frying.

As a convenient and thoroughly enjoyable way to cook, deep-frying turns up in almost every national cuisine. India has its samosas and gulab jamun, South East Asian countries prize their tempura, wontons and spring rolls and Americans down corn dogs and Southern fried chicken with relish. In Europe each country has its deep-fried treats from French beignets and Spanish churros to Italian fritto misto and great British fish and chips. Cooks have long valued these dishes as an important part of their culinary heritage, as recipes have passed down the generations.

RIGHT Apple funnel cake

If you reluctantly banished your deep fat fryer to the garage several years ago, maybe it's time to dust it off and let it back in the kitchen. The recipes in this book aim to show you that deep-fried food can be part of a sensible, balanced diet, it needn't be over-rich and horribly unhealthy but light, tasty and there to be enjoyed. So let's get frying tonight!

BE SAFE WHEN DEEP-FRYING

Of paramount importance, so let's talk about this first. It might be stating the obvious but it is imperative to take extra care when you deep-fry in your kitchen at home. We've all read about the horrific consequences of chip pans catching fire and none of us wants to be part of those statistics. Electric deep-fat fryers are the safest way to deep-fry as they are solidly built, difficult to tip over and have a tight-fitting lid that keeps the hot oil covered while the food is cooking. If you have small children, pets that might get under your feet or you deep-fry regularly, it's well worth investing in one of these.

However, it is perfectly safe to use a saucepan and frying basket as long as you follow a few common sense guidelines:

- Never leave a pan of hot fat unattended. If the phone rings and you've just put food in the fryer, lift the basket clear of the oil, turn off the heat source and continue when you've finished the call (remembering to reheat the oil back up to temperature first).
- Avoid over-filling the saucepan with oil. It should not be more than half-full and there should be roughly 7.5 cm/3 in between the oil and the top of the pan. Remember the oil level will rise when you add food.
- Never carry an open pan of hot fat across the kitchen. Slide the pan carefully to the back of the hob and leave the fat cool down.

- When using a saucepan for deep-frying, turn the handle inwards so there is no risk of you catching it with your sleeve and overturning the pan.
- Keep a fire extinguisher or fire blanket within easy reach should an accident happen and the oil catch fire. Turn off the heat source and never attempt to put out the fire by dousing it with water as this will cause the flames to spread.
- Avoid putting wet food into hot oil or it will splash and spit.
- If deep-frying in a saucepan, choose a pan where the base is larger than the hob plate so any splashes do not come in contact with an electric hot plate or gas flame.

ABOVE Cooks in Asian countries not only use their wok for stir-frying, but also for creating deep-fried dishes such as crispy fried seaweed.

ABOVE When deep frying with a wok, make sure it is safely secured to a special stand to avoid wobbling.

TYPES OF DEEP FRYERS

ELECTRIC DEEP-FAT FRYERS

These vary considerably in size and price but all should have a filter to keep frying odours at bay, a thermostat to heat the oil to the correct temperature and a basket that can be lowered and raised easily. Other features to look out for are a built-in timer, non-stick coating, viewing window, variable heat control, dishwasher safe basket and interior liner and a basket that can be lowered and raised without opening the lid.

WOK

In Asian countries, cooks use a wok for every method of cooking, including deep-frying. Whilst its unique shape of narrow base and wide top make it ideal for deep-frying, it is essential that the rounded bottom of the wok is securely anchored on a special stand so there is no risk of it wobbling or tipping over when filled with hot oil.

LARGE SAUCEPAN WITH FRYING BASKET

The saucepan should be deep and made of either cast iron or thick metal with a heavy base. The frying basket should have hooks (or a similar device) that will fit over the top edge of a saucepan allowing excess oil to drip back into the pan before the food is tipped out of the basket and drained on absorbent kitchen paper.

LARGE, DEEP FRYING PAN

This can be used for deep-frying small items of food such as croutons or bite-size fritters that only require an inch or so of oil for them to be immersed.

FONDUE SET

Ideal for table cooking when you're planning an informal dinner with friends. As well as the classic fondue of cheese and bourguignon made with beef, the pot can also be used for Japanese tempura.

RIGHT You don't have to own an electric deep-fat fryer to create delicious fried treats. You can also use a fondue set or a frying pan.

WHICH FAT TO USE FOR DEEP-FRYING?

Oil is the most popular fat for deep-frying food, although solid white vegetable fat or lard could also be used. Different oils have different smoke points, i.e. the temperature to which the oil can be heated before it starts to smoke, as follows:

Soya, grapeseed, safflower, groundnut (peanut)	-	225°C/430°F
Rape seed (canola)	-	210°C/405°F
Olive, sesame, corn	-	200°C/400°F
Sunflower	-	190°C/375°F

Oil marked simply 'Vegetable Oil' will be made up of a mix of different oils, eg corn, rape seed and soya. Excellent for deep-frying, it has a high smoke point, no intrusive flavour and, being a mix of oils, is cheaper than single ingredient oils.

Olive and sesame oils are rarely used for deep-frying because of their strong taste. However, when cooking some Mediterranean or Chinese dishes these oils are used specifically to add their flavour to the dish.

If frying with olive oil, use ordinary olive oil or olive pomace oil, both of which have the same smoke and flash points as corn oil and are very stable at high temperatures. Extra virgin olive oils should be avoided as although most are stable at high temperatures some may not be. One of the advantages of ordinary olive oil is that it is actually more stable than other vegetable oils because of its anti-oxidant content (mostly vitamin E), some of which survives the refining process. It can therefore be used more times in a deep-fat fryer than other oils, as long as it is filtered each time to get rid of burnt bits of food and its temperature is thermostatically controlled (see Re-using Oil below). Olive pomace oil (oil extracted from the pomace or solid residue after olive oil has been pressed out and then refined) does not contain any vitamin E but is still a good oil to deep-fry with and is cheaper than ordinary olive oil.

Although the majority of oils have higher smoke points than 190°C/375°F, it is dangerous to heat oil for deep-frying above this temperature. If the oil does get too hot, remove the pan from the heat to allow it to cool to the required temperature.

When frying food at high altitudes, the recommended oil temperature should be raised by 25°F.

BELOW There's nothing like cooking your own home-made French fries.

RE-USING OIL

Oil can be re-used several times. After frying, allow the oil to cool completely before draining it through a fine sieve or coffee filter paper to remove any particles of food before pouring it back into the bottle.

If the oil starts to smoke or becomes dark in colour, it has been heated to too high a temperature and must be discard as it will give food an unpleasant burnt flavour. When oil gets too hot, it begins to oxidise and break down, a chemical reaction caused by the heating process.

Fish can taint frying oil especially if it has a strong flavour so, if this happens, keep the oil separate and make sure that you do not use it for frying other foods.

STEPS TO PERFECT DEEP-FRYING

- With the exception of chips, which are only cooked for a brief time, food needs a protective coating before it is deep-fried. This coating will protect delicate ingredients and stop the food absorbing too much oil (see Coatings section below).
- Food with a high water content, such as fish, should only be coated about 30 minutes before frying. By leaving it to stand, the coating will absorb moisture from the food and prevent it becoming crisp.
- Oil needs to be heated to the correct temperature before food can be fried. If your deep-fryer doesn't have a built-in thermostat, it is worth investing in a cooking thermometer. Alternatively, you can calculate the temperature of the oil by adding a cube of bread and checking how long it takes the bread to sizzle and brown. Timings for this method are:

BELOW Spicy samosas make a delicious snack.

Oil temperature	Time it takes bread to sizzle and brown
Low - 160°C/325°F	60 seconds
Moderate – 180°C/350°F	40 seconds
Hot – 190°C/375°F	20 seconds

BELOW Tempura prawns with
barbecue sauce served on a bed
of egg noodles.

- Before frying, dip the empty frying basket in the hot oil first so food doesn't stick to it. Cook food in small batches as overfilling the basket will encourage pieces of food to stick together and cause the temperature of the oil to drop. When adding food to the basket, make sure each piece has space around it.
- Add ingredients to hot oil a few pieces at a time using tongs or a similar utensil and avoid dropping anything in from a height as it will cause the oil to rise up in the pan or spit.
- Drain food as soon as it is cooked on to a plate lined with a double thickness of absorbent kitchen paper. When frying in batches, drain the food as it cooks and keep warm in a single layer in a low oven with the oven door slightly open so air can circulate. Avoid covering the food as this will create steam and make it go soggy. Dust deep-fried food with salt or sugar to help absorb any oil remaining on the surface.

TROUBLE SHOOTING—WHAT WENT WRONG?

FOOD IS PALE IN COLOUR AND COATING HEAVY AND GREASY
- Undercooking
- Food chilled for too long after coating
- Oil not heated to a high enough temperature

FOOD HAS GONE SOGGY
- Not fried immediately after coating
- Food covered whilst being kept warm

COATING HAS BROWNED TOO MUCH BEFORE
THE FOOD IS COOKED
- Oil has become too hot
- Coating has too much added salt or sugar

FRITTERS OR BEIGNETS BURST
- Oil too hot causing fruit or other filling to burst

COATINGS

A coating is necessary to protect delicate ingredients and stop food absorbing too much oil as it fries. Coatings can be in the form of a batter, breadcrumbs (dry or fresh), matzo meal, dry polenta, seasoned flour, pastry (choux, filo, puff, Chinese spring roll wrappers) or semolina.

Batters made with whole eggs are thick and rich, whereas those made with egg white only will be light and crisp.

Before coating with a batter, food should be dusted with flour first so the batter has something to stick to, otherwise most of it will simply slide off. Food with a dry coating such as breadcrumbs, matzo meal or polenta, needs to be dusted first with flour and then brushed with beaten egg before the crumbs are pressed over.

For a dish like Chicken Kiev where it is important the garlic butter and herb filling doesn't leak out during cooking, the chicken breasts are given a double coating of flour, beaten egg and crumbs to ensure a tight seal.

ABOVE Before you place your food in the deep-fat fryer for frying, dip the basket in the oil first so that the food doesn't stick to the wire when you place it in to cook.

BATTERS

All batters (except Tempura batter) should be left to stand for 30 minutes to 1 hour (or longer) before using as this allows the gluten in the flour to swell and gives a lighter batter. If after standing the batter has thickened too much, stir in a little extra water, or lager if it is a beer batter. If adding whisked egg whites, fold these in after the batter has been left to stand.

Tempura Batter

2 egg yolks
250 ml/9 fl oz iced water
200 g/7 oz plain flour

Put the egg yolks in a bowl and whisk in the water, beating until frothy. Sift in the flour and beat until just combined. The batter should have the consistency of single cream, so if it is too thick add a little more water. As this batter is very light, it should be made and used straight away.

Yeast Batter

7 g/¼-oz sachet of easy-blend
    dried yeast
Pinch of sugar
75 g/3 oz plain flour
100 ml/4 fl oz warm water
50 ml/2 fl oz warm milk

Sprinkle the yeast and sugar over the flour in a bowl. Stir until well blended. Pour in the water and milk and stir to make a smooth batter. Cover and leave to stand for 1 hour until frothy. Stir before using.

Simple Flour and Water Batter

200 g/7 oz self-raising flour
Pinch of bicarbonate of soda
300 ml/½ pt cold water

Sift the flour and bicarbonate of soda into a bowl, make a well in the centre and pour in the water. Whisk to make a smooth batter. Leave to stand for 1 hour before using.

Beer Batter – No 1

100 g/4 oz self-raising flour
Pinch of salt
½ tsp baking powder
8 fl oz (225 ml) light lager beer

Sift the flour, salt and baking powder into a bowl. Make a well in the centre and add half the beer. Gradually whisk this into the dry ingredients and then whisk in the rest of the beer until you have a smooth batter. Leave to stand for 1 hour before using.

Beer Batter – No 2

225 g/8 oz self-raising flour
300 ml/½ pt light lager beer
Salt and pepper
1 egg white

Sift the flour into a bowl, make a well in the centre and add half the beer. Gradually whisk this into the flour and then whisk in the rest of the beer until smooth. Season with salt and pepper. Leave to stand for at least 1 hour. Just before using, whisk the egg white until standing in soft peaks and fold into the batter.

Deep-fried Turkeys

- In recent years, more and more cooks in America's Deep South have begun deep-frying their Thanksgiving turkeys. Fans of this method of cooking say it's fun, easy and hassle-free and that once you've tasted the moist, succulent flesh of a deep-fried turkey you won't go back to oven-roasting ever again.

- Critics are more cautious, pointing out that deep-frying such a large bird is dangerous and a disaster waiting to happen and regular reports of burns, fires and serious accidents tend to give credence to their views.

- However, any cooking method for turkey requires care and attention and deep-frying is no different. Stick to the recommended guidelines and safety rules and you can cook a bird this way with confidence.

- For a 4.5-5.4 kg/10-12 lb turkey you will need a large pot, a high output heat source and a special long-stem temperature probe, so it's worth investing in a special 36-40 quart fryer from a kitchen equipment store. Each make will come with its own cooking and safety instructions so it is essential to read these before you begin.

- If you buy a frozen turkey, it must defrost completely before it is cooked, partly because any ice crystals left in the body cavity will slow the cooking process down but, more importantly, if you lower a frozen or partly-thawed turkey into hot oil the moisture in it will cause the oil to spit dangerously and boil over.

- To ensure a turkey is completely defrosted, place the bird in its plastic wrapper on a tray in the refrigerator and leave it there for 24 hours for every 2.3 kg/5 lb the bird weighs.

- When ready to deep-fry it, avoid stuffing the turkey and season it instead using a commercially produced spice mix or sauce and injector or your own combination of spices rubbed inside the bird (avoid seasoning the outside of the turkey as this will fall off when it goes into the oil).

- Although the turkey must be completely submerged in the frying oil, it is imperative not to overfill the fryer as when you lower in the bird, the hot oil could overflow. To calculate how much oil to use, place the turkey in the empty fryer and pour in enough water to cover it by a couple of inches. Lift the bird out and measure the water to determine the quantity of oil you need. Any oil with a high smoke point can be used, although groundnut (peanut) oil is the favourite of many cooks who say its flavour best compliments the turkey flesh.

- When ready to fry, heat the measured oil in the fryer to 160–180ºC/325–350ºF. Weigh the turkey to calculate the cooking time – the recommended time is 3-5 minutes per 450 g/1 lb, depending on the size and plumpness of the bird.

- Blot the turkey completely dry with absorbent kitchen paper, place it on the rack or in the frying basket breast side down and slowly lower it into the hot oil. Fry the turkey for the calculated time and use a meat thermometer or probe to ascertain when the internal temperature reaches 82ºC/180ºF. To do this, lift the turkey out of the fryer and insert the thermometer into the thickest part of the thigh. If the required temperature has not been reached, return the turkey to the oil and continue cooking.

- Once the turkey is done, remove it carefully from the oil and drain it on a platter lined with absorbent paper. Leave it to stand for 15-20 minutes before carving to allow the juices to run back into the flesh, making it juicier and easier to carve.

Watchpoints to Deep-fry a Turkey Safely:

- Make sure the fryer is sitting on a completely flat surface with plenty of space around it – fry outdoors for preference, but note that oil dripped on a concrete surface will leave a stain.

- Wear thick oven gloves to protect your hands.

- Never leave the fryer unattended whilst the oil is heating or the turkey cooking.

- Keep children and pets well away from the frying area.

- Keep a fire extinguisher close by.

- Continue to be vigilant after cooking by leaving the oil to cool down to a safe temperature before you attempt to drain the fryer.

FINAL WATCHPOINTS

- Always protect your hand with an oven mitt when you add food to hot fat.
- Avoid deep-frying large pieces of food from frozen. Thaw them thoroughly first and blot with absorbent kitchen paper until completely dry. Small items can be deep-fried from frozen but wipe off any surface moisture and fry at low-moderate temperature (160–180°C/325–350°F) so they cook through thoroughly.
- Extra care needs to be taken when deep-frying poultry. Depending on the thickness of the meat, fry at a low-moderate temperature (160°C/325°F) and test the thickest part of the flesh for done-ness with a temperature probe. A large chicken joint or whole bird should never be deep-fried whilst still frozen. Once immersed in the hot oil, it would cause the oil to boil up and possibly explode.
- Deep-fried food will be very hot straight from the fryer and the denser the food the longer it will retain its heat. When serving deep-fried food as party nibbles, allow items to cool a little before handing round to your guests.
- Anyone with an allergy to peanuts will suffer a similar allergic reaction to food deep-fried in peanut oil.

BELOW Spiced new potatoes are excellent served with curried mayonnaise.

1 | snacks

Every cuisine has its own deep-fried snacks and these recipes are just a few of the well-loved favourites that turn up as street food around the world. Walk down a busy street in cities as diverse as Mumbai, Mexico City, Athens or Bangkok or stroll through a bustling West Indian market and you'll find it hard to ignore the seductive smells drifting your way from the food stalls set up on every other corner. Crisp pastry parcels with spicy fillings turn up as spring rolls in China and Singapore, as samosas in India or spanakopittes (filo triangles stuffed with spinach and feta cheese) in Greece, while more substantial treats might be Maryland chicken or Louisiana corn dogs. Deep-fried snacks make great party food for all ages and can be served in twists of paper or on paper plates wrapped in mini napkins to save on washing up.

Greek Cheese Pastries

CRISP TRIANGLES OF FILO PASTRY FILLED WITH A TANGY MIX OF CHEESE, EGG AND HERBS. WHEN WORKING WITH FILO, USE ONE SHEET AT A TIME AND KEEP THE OTHERS COVERED WITH PLASTIC WRAP OR A DAMP CLOTH SO THEY DON'T DRY OUT AND BECOME BRITTLE.

MAKES 24

250 g/9 oz feta cheese
1 egg, beaten
1 Tbsp chopped fresh mint
½ tsp dried oregano
½ tsp dried thyme
Freshly ground black pepper
8 sheets of filo pastry, measuring
    30 x 19 cm/12 x 7 in
1 egg, beaten
Oil or beaten egg for brushing

1 Crumble the feta into a bowl, add the beaten egg, mint, oregano and thyme and season with freshly ground black pepper. Mash the ingredients together.

2 Unwrap the pastry sheets and place on a board. Brush one sheet lightly with oil and cut lengthways into 3 long strips.

3 Put a teaspoon of the cheese mixture at the corner of one strip. Fold the corner over the filling and keep folding over and over up the strip to make a triangular pastry, pressing the edges together to seal. Repeat until you have made 24 pastries using the remaining filling and filo sheets.

4 Heat oil for deep-frying to 180°C/350°F and fry the pastries in batches for 2 minutes or until golden brown and crisp. Drain and serve hot or cold.

Corn Dogs

A FAVOURITE STREET FOOD SOLD FROM FOOD CARTS ACROSS AMERICA. ALTHOUGH FRANKFURTERS ORIGINATED IN GERMANY, THEY WERE DUBBED "DOGS" IN THE USA AFTER A CARTOON POOCH WITH A SLIMLINE BODY BECAME A CULT FIGURE. IF YOU USE INSTANT OR QUICK-COOK POLENTA FOR MAKING THE BATTER, IT WILL ABSORB LIQUID MUCH QUICKER THAN ORDINARY POLENTA AND THE BATTER WILL BECOME TOO THICK. IF THIS HAPPENS, SIMPLY STIR IN EXTRA MILK OR WATER.

MAKES 8

50 g/2 oz fine yellow cornmeal
　　or polenta
75 g/3 oz plain flour, plus extra
　　for dusting
¼ tsp bicarbonate of soda
¼ tsp mild chilli powder
150 ml/¼ pt buttermilk or thin
　　natural yoghurt
50 ml/2 fl oz milk
1 egg
8 frankfurters
Oil for deep-frying

To serve:
Mustard and tomato ketchup

1　Soak 8 wooden skewers in water for 30 minutes so they don't burn in the hot oil.

2　In a bowl, mix together the cornmeal or polenta, 75 g/3 oz of plain flour, bicarbonate of soda and chilli powder. In a jug, beat the buttermilk or yoghurt, milk and egg together and pour into the dry ingredients, stirring until smooth.

3　Pat the frankfurters dry with kitchen paper and dust them with flour. Push a skewer though the length of each, leaving 5 cm/2 in sticking out. Heat oil for deep-frying to 190°C/375°F.

4　Dip the frankfurters in the batter so they are evenly coated, shaking gently so any excess drips off.

5　Slowly lower four of the frankfurters into the pan – don't drop them in too quickly or they will sink and stick to the basket – and fry for about 4 minutes until golden brown, turning over after 2 minutes. Drain and fry the remaining frankfurters in the same way.

6　Serve the Corn Dogs with mustard and tomato ketchup.

Vegetable Crisps ILLUSTRATED RIGHT

PARSNIPS, CARROTS, PLANTAINS AND SWEET POTATOES CAN ALL BE TURNED INTO VEGETABLE CRISPS TO SERVE WITH DRINKS. IF YOU HAVE A MANDOLINE OR SLICING ATTACHMENT FOR A FOOD PROCESSOR, CUT THE VEGETABLES INTO WAFER-THIN SLICES, IF NOT SHAVE THEM INTO RIBBONS USING A VEGETABLE PEELER.

SERVES 4 TO 6

900 g/2 lb mixed vegetables,
    e.g., parsnips, carrots, sweet
    potatoes
Oil for deep-frying
Salt

1 Peel the vegetables and cut into wafer-thin rounds or ribbons. Pat dry with kitchen paper.

2 Heat oil for deep-frying to 180°C/350°F and fry the vegetables in batches, without over-crowding the basket. Shake it from time to time so the chips don't stick together.

3 Cook for 3 to 4 minutes or until lightly browned. Drain, cool and sprinkle with salt before serving.

Hot and Spicy Pasta Crunch

SERVE THIS CRUNCHY, SPICY PASTA WITH PRE-DINNER DRINKS AT A PARTY OR FAMILY GET TOGETHER.

MAKES 250 G/9 OZ

250 g/9 oz mixed pasta shapes,
    e.g., bows and spirals
1 Tbsp plain flour
2 tsp paprika
1 tsp hot chilli powder
1 tsp caraway seeds
Oil for deep-frying

1 Cook the pasta shapes in a large pan of boiling water for 8 to 10 minutes or until tender. Drain and run cold water through the sieve to cool the pasta.

2 Drain thoroughly, transfer the pasta to a bowl and add the flour, paprika, chilli powder and caraway seeds. Toss so all the shapes are coated in the flour and spices.

3 Heat oil for deep-frying to 180°C/350°F and fry the pasta, a little at a time, until slightly golden. Drain well on kitchen paper.

4 Reheat the oil to 190°C/375°F and fry the pasta again in two or three batches until golden brown and crisp. Drain and sprinkle with salt.

Curried Beef Rolls

LARGER VERSIONS OF THESE CRISP FILO ROLLS CAN BE MADE AS A LUNCH OR SUPPER DISH AND
SERVED WITH A CRISP MIXED SALAD. WHEN SERVING WITH DRINKS, PILE THE WARM ROLLS IN A
PLATTER AND ACCOMPANY WITH A TOMATO DIPPING SAUCE.

MAKES 16

1 shallot
½ red pepper
½ green pepper
Oil for deep-frying, plus an
    extra 2 Tbsp
225 g/8 oz lean minced beef
1 Tbsp curry paste
2 Tbsp tomato purée
225 ml/8 fl oz beef stock
Salt and pepper
8 sheets of filo pastry,
    measuring 30 x 19 cm/
    12 x 7 in
1 egg, beaten

1 Peel and finely chop the shallot, deseed and finely chop the peppers.

2 Heat 2 tablespoons of oil in a frying pan, add the shallot and peppers and fry gently for 5 minutes until softened. Increase the heat under the pan, add the mince and fry until browned, breaking up any lumps of meat with a spoon.

3 Add the curry paste, tomato purée and stock, lower the heat and simmer gently with the pan uncovered for 15 minutes until most of the liquid has evaporated and the mixture is quite dry. Season and leave to cool.

4 Cut the filo sheets in half across the centre to give 16 squares. Brush the edges of one square with beaten egg and spoon a little of the meat mixture in the centre. Fold in the sides and roll the filo around the filling, sealing tightly. Repeat with the remaining pastry sheets and filling to make 16 rolls.

5 Heat oil for deep-frying to 180°C/350°F and fry the rolls in batches for about 3 minutes or until golden and crisp. Drain and serve warm.

Goat's Cheese Rosti

THE ROSTI CAN BE COOKED AHEAD OF TIME AND FROZEN UNTIL NEEDED. TO REHEAT, SPREAD OUT THE STILL-FROZEN ROSTI ON A BAKING SHEET AND REHEAT IN A HOT OVEN FOR 10 MINUTES BEFORE ADDING THE TOPPING.

MAKES ABOUT 24

450 g/1 lb potatoes
4 spring onions
2 eggs, beaten
Salt and pepper
Oil for deep-frying
100 g/4 oz soft goat's cheese, or
    another soft cheese
Cherry tomatoes and flat-leaf
    parsley sprigs, to garnish

1 Peel the potatoes and grate into a bowl. Pour over cold water to cover and set aside for 1 hour. Finely chop the spring onions and set aside.

2 Drain the grated potato and pat dry on kitchen paper. Return to the wiped out bowl and mix in the spring onions, beaten egg and seasoning.

3 Heat oil for deep-frying to 180°C/350°F and carefully add tablespoons of the potato mixture. Cook in batches for 2 to 3 minutes or until crisp and golden brown. Drain and allow to cool slightly.

4 Spoon a little goat's cheese onto each rosti, pressing it down lightly, and top with cherry tomato quarters and parsley.

Prawn and Chilli Toasts

THE PRAWN PASTE CAN BE PREPARED AHEAD OF TIME AND STORED IN A COVERED BOWL IN THE REFRIGERATOR UNTIL NEEDED, BUT THE TOASTS ARE BEST IF COOKED JUST BEFORE SERVING. SERVE WITH PLUM SAUCE OR ANOTHER ORIENTAL DIP.

MAKES 24

450 g/1 lb raw prawns
4 spring onions
1 red chilli
1 egg white, lightly beaten
1 tsp finely grated root ginger
2 tsp light soy sauce
1 tsp sugar
1 tsp sesame oil
Salt and pepper
6 large thin-cut slices of white
    bread, crusts removed
3 Tbsp sesame seeds
Oil for deep-frying

1 Peel, devein and roughly chop the prawns. Chop the spring onions, deseed and chop the chilli.

2 Place the prawns, spring onions and chilli in a food processor and blend to a paste. Transfer to a bowl and stir in the egg white, ginger, soy sauce, sugar and sesame oil. Season with salt and pepper.

3 Cut each slice of bread into four squares and spread thickly with the prawn paste. Sprinkle the sesame seeds on top.

4 Heat oil for deep-frying to 180°C/350°F and fry the toasts three or four at a time, paste-side down, for 2 minutes. Flip them over and fry for a further 2 minutes or until golden brown and crisp.

5 Drain and serve warm with plum sauce or a similar dip.

Fried Bananas in Coconut Batter

A POPULAR STREET SNACK IN THE FAR EAST, PARTICULARLY THAILAND WHERE ROADSIDE CHEFS TOSS THE CRISP BANANA FRITTERS IN WOKS OF CRACKLING OIL. SERVE ON THEIR OWN AS A SNACK OR AS A DESSERT WITH VANILLA ICE CREAM. CHOOSE BANANAS THAT ARE SLIGHTLY UNDER-RIPE SO THEY DON'T BECOME MUSHY WHEN COOKED.

SERVES 4

100 g/4 oz plain flour, plus extra
    to dust
½ tsp ground mixed spice
50 g/2 oz caster sugar, plus extra
    to dust
Pinch of salt
225 ml/8 fl oz coconut milk
4 medium, under-ripe bananas
Oil for deep-frying

1 Sift 100 g/4 oz of flour and the mixed spice into a bowl and stir in the sugar and salt. Make a well in the centre of the dry ingredients, pour in the coconut milk and mix to a smooth batter. Set aside for 30 minutes.

2 Peel the bananas and cut into 1-cm/½-in thick strips, about 7.5 cm/3 in long.

3 Heat oil for deep-frying to 180°C/350°F. Dust the banana strips with flour, dip in the batter and deep-fry in batches for about 2 minutes until golden. Drain and serve dusted with extra caster sugar.

Maryland Chicken Nuggets with Corn Fritters

FINGER LICKIN' MORSELS OF SUCCULENT CHICKEN WITH THE CLASSIC MARYLAND ACCOMPANIMENTS OF CORN FRITTERS, BACON ROLLS AND FRIED BANANAS. SERVE AS A SNACK OR IN PAPER CONES AT A PARTY WITH BOWLS OF MUSTARD AND KETCHUP FOR DIPPING.

SERVES 4

2 chicken breasts, skinned and
   boned
50 g/2 oz fresh breadcrumbs
1 Tbsp ground almonds
1 tsp dried thyme
75 g/3 oz plain flour
1 egg, beaten

Corn fritters:
50 g/2 oz plain flour
1 egg, beaten
198 g/7 oz can sweetcorn
   kernels with peppers
2 Tbsp milk

To serve:
2 bananas
4 streaky bacon rashers
Oil for deep and shallow frying

1 Cut each chicken breast into four pieces across the grain of the meat. Mix together the breadcrumbs, ground almonds and thyme and spread out on a plate.

2 Dust the chicken pieces in flour, brush with beaten egg and coat in the breadcrumb mixture. Chill for 1 hour.

3 To make the fritters, sift the flour into a bowl, add the egg, sweetcorn and milk and stir until evenly mixed.

4 Peel and cut each banana into four pieces. Halve the bacon rashers and roll them up.

5 Heat oil for deep-frying to 180°C/350°F and fry the chicken pieces in two batches for 5 minutes until golden brown.

6 Meanwhile, heat oil for shallow frying in a large frying pan and drop in tablespoonfuls of the fritter mixture. Fry for 2 minutes on each side until golden. Grill the bacon rolls for 5 minutes until golden brown and crisp.

7 Drain the chicken and fritters and keep warm in a low oven. Dust the banana pieces in flour and fry in the pan used for the fritters until lightly golden. Drain and serve with the chicken, fritters and bacon rolls.

Spicy Vegetable Rolls with Chilli Peanut Dip

IF YOU MAKE THE DIP AHEAD OF TIME AND IT THICKENS TOO MUCH ON COOLING, STIR IN EXTRA HOT WATER TO BRING IT TO THE RIGHT CONSISTENCY.

MAKES 10

Rolls:
225 g/8 oz sweet potatoes
1 medium cauliflower
1 leek
4 medium tomatoes
2 Tbsp oil, plus extra for deep-frying
1 tsp ground turmeric
1 tsp ground cumin
2 tsp ground coriander
50 g/2 oz frozen peas
10 sheets of filo pastry, measuring 30 x 19 cm/ 12 x 7 in

Dip:
1 shallot
1 garlic clove
2 Tbsp oil
4 Tbsp crunchy peanut butter
1 Tbsp creamed coconut (grated if from a solid block)
1 tsp hot chilli sauce
1 tsp brown sugar

1 To make the rolls, peel the sweet potatoes and cut into small dice. Trim the cauliflower and divide into tiny florets. Trim and finely slice the leek. Peel, deseed and dice the tomatoes. Cook the sweet potato and cauliflower in a pan of boiling water for 5 minutes or until just tender. Drain and set aside.

2 Heat 2 tablespoons of oil in a frying pan, add the leek and fry until softened. Sprinkle in the spices and cook for 2 minutes and then add the sweet potato, cauliflower, tomatoes and frozen peas and fry for 3 minutes. Remove from the heat and leave to cool.

3 Place a sheet of filo pastry on a board and spoon a little of the filling down the centre. Dampen the edges and roll the filo around the filling to enclose, tucking in the sides. Repeat with the remaining filo sheets to make 10 rolls.

4 Heat oil for deep-frying to 180°C/350°F and fry the rolls in two batches for 4 to 5 minutes or until golden and crisp.

5 While the rolls are cooking, make the dip. Peel and finely chop the shallot, peel and finely chop the garlic. Heat the oil in a pan and gently fry the shallot and garlic until golden. Stir in the peanut butter, creamed coconut, chilli sauce and brown sugar and gradually blend in 300 ml/½ pt of water. Heat through without boiling. Drain the rolls and serve with the dip.

Fish Sticks

ANY FIRM WHITE FISH COULD BE USED BUT THICKER FILLETS SUCH AS COD, MONKFISH OR HADDOCK WORK BETTER THAN FLAT FISH LIKE PLAICE OR SOLE. ALLOW THE FISH TO MARINATE FOR ABOUT 20 MINUTES BEFORE FRYING.

SERVES 4

2 garlic cloves
½ tsp salt
2 tsp grated fresh root ginger
Juice of 2 limes
450 g/1 lb white fish fillets
Flour, to dust
1 tsp dried thyme
½ tsp paprika
1 quantity of Beer Batter No 2
**   or Simple Flour and Water**
**   Batter (see page 14)**
Oil for deep-frying

1 Peel and crush the garlic with the salt. Mix with the ginger and lime juice.

2 Skin the fish, remove any bones and cut into 2.5 cm/1 in sticks across the grain of the flesh.

3 Place the fish in a shallow dish, spread with the garlic and ginger mix and set aside for 20 minutes.

4 Dust the fish sticks with flour. Stir the thyme and paprika into the batter and heat oil for deep-frying to 180°C/350°F.

5 Dip the fish in the batter and fry in batches for 2 to 3 minutes until golden brown and crisp. Drain and serve with ketchup or mayonnaise and lemon wedges to squeeze over.

Herby-crumbed Mushrooms with Mustard Mayonnaise ILLUSTRATED RIGHT

TWIST OUT THE MUSHROOM STALKS OR LEAVE THEM IN PLACE, AS YOU PREFER. IF YOU DO REMOVE THEM, THEY CAN BE CHOPPED AND ADDED TO A STOCK, GRAVY OR SAUCE FOR ANOTHER RECIPE.

SERVES 4

20 medium-sized cup
    mushrooms
Flour, to dust
Salt and pepper
2 eggs, beaten
175 g/6 oz fresh white
    breadcrumbs
1 tsp dried thyme
½ tsp dried marjoram
Oil for deep-frying
6 Tbsp mayonnaise
2 tsp wholegrain mustard
Fresh thyme sprigs, to garnish

1 Rinse the mushrooms and pat dry with absorbent paper. Dust with seasoned flour and brush with the beaten egg, making sure the gills and stalks are well coated.

2 Mix the breadcrumbs with the thyme and marjoram and press over the mushrooms until evenly covered. Chill for 30 minutes.

3 Heat oil for deep-frying to 180°C/350°F and fry the mushrooms in batches for 3 to 4 minutes until golden brown. Drain.

4 Stir the mayonnaise and mustard together and serve with the hot mushrooms and some fresh thyme sprigs.

Fried Cheese and Ham Sandwiches

INSTEAD OF MOZZARELLA YOU COULD USE EITHER GRUYÈRE OR EMMENTHAL CHEESE TO MAKE THE SANDWICHES AS BOTH BECOME DELICIOUSLY CREAMY WHEN COOKED. WHEN COATING THE BREAD IN BEATEN EGG, BRUSH PLENTY DOWN THE SIDES TO MAKE A TIGHT SEAL OR THE CHEESE WILL BUBBLE OUT INTO THE FRYER.

SERVES 4

200 g/7 oz mozzarella
8 large slices of medium-sliced
    bread
4 tsp smooth mustard
4 thin slices of ham
Oil for deep-frying
2 eggs, beaten

1 Cut the mozzarella into thin slices. Spread the bread with the mustard and cut the slices in half.

2 Sandwich the bread with the mozzarella and ham, making sure none of the cheese slices are poking out the sides of the sandwiches.

3 Heat oil for deep-frying to 180°C/350°F. Dip the sandwiches in the beaten egg until well coated and fry in the hot oil for 1 to 2 minutes or until golden brown on both sides. Drain and serve at once with chutney or pickle.

Stamp and Go

THESE JAMAICAN COD CAKES GOT THEIR NAME FROM THE FOOD STALLS WHO USED TO SELL THEM WRAPPED IN PAPER WITH THE WORD 'PAID' STAMPED ON THE OUTSIDE – HENCE 'STAMP AND GO'. IN DAYS GONE BY COD WAS SALTED TO PRESERVE IT BUT, DESPITE THE ADVENT OF REFRIGERATION, 'BACALAO', KNOWN AS SALT COD IN THE CARIBBEAN ISLANDS, IS STILL POPULAR TODAY.

SERVES 4

250 g/9 oz salt cod
2 garlic cloves
2 bay leaves
1 onion
2 Tbsp oil, plus extra for deep-frying
100 g/4 oz plain flour
1 tsp baking powder
1 egg, separated
100 ml/4 fl oz milk
1 Tbsp melted butter
2 Tbsp chopped fresh coriander
1 Tbsp snipped chives
Pinch of cayenne pepper

1 Soak the salt cod in cold water for 24 hours, changing the oil several times. Drain the fish, place in a saucepan and cover with cold water. Peel the garlic cloves and add one to the pan with the bay leaves.

2 Simmer for 15 minutes, then drain the cod and leave to cool. Remove the skin and any bones and flake the flesh.

3 Peel and finely chop the onion. Crush the second clove of garlic. Heat 2 tablespoons of oil in a pan and fry the onion and garlic until soft and lightly golden.

4 Sift the flour and baking powder into a bowl and beat in the egg yolk, milk, melted butter, coriander, chives and cayenne. Add the cod and fried onion and garlic and stir together until well mixed. Leave to stand in the refrigerator for 1 to 2 hours.

5 Whisk the egg white until standing in soft peaks and fold into the cod mixture.

6 Heat oil for deep-frying to 180°C/350°F. Using a large spoon, drop small balls of the batter into the oil and fry for 3 to 4 minutes until golden brown. Drain and serve hot.

Tuna Empanadas

IN MEXICO, THESE TORTILLA PARCELS WOULD MOST LIKELY BE STUFFED WITH A SALSA MIXTURE OF SWEETCORN AND MUSHROOMS BUT IN GALICIA IN NORTH-WEST SPAIN, TUNA IS A POPULAR FILLING.

MAKES 12

450 g/1 lb fresh tuna steaks
2 medium tomatoes
1 green pepper
2 shallots
2 Tbsp olive oil
2 Tbsp chopped fresh parsley
4 Tbsp soured cream
12 wheatflour tortillas, about
    15 cm/6 in in diameter
Beaten egg for brushing
Oil for deep-frying

1 Grill the tuna steaks until just cooked, remove any skin and flake the flesh into a bowl.

2 Skin, deseed and finely dice the tomatoes, deseed and finely chop the pepper, peel and finely chop the shallots.

3 Heat the olive oil in a pan and fry the pepper and shallots until softened. Remove from the heat and stir in the tomatoes, flaked tuna, parsley and soured cream. Allow to cool.

4 Divide the tuna mix between the tortillas, brush the edges with beaten egg and fold in half to make semi-circular parcels, pressing the edges together to seal.

5 Heat oil for deep-frying to 180°C/350°F and fry the empanadas in batches for 3 to 4 minutes until golden and crisp on both sides. Drain and serve warm.

Black-eyed Pea Fritters with Prawns

THESE SPICY LITTLE FRITTERS ARE FAMILIAR STREET SNACKS IN THE BAHIA REGION OF BRAZIL BUT HAVE THEIR ORIGINS IN AFRICAN SLAVE FOOD. KNOWN AS ACARAJE, THE FRITTERS WOULD BE FRIED IN DENDE (PALM) OIL IN BRAZIL BUT MORE READILY AVAILABLE OILS SUCH AS CORN OR VEGETABLE CAN BE USED INSTEAD. DRIED PRAWNS ARE AVAILABLE FROM ORIENTAL SUPERMARKETS.

MAKES 16

225 g/8 oz dried black-eyed
    peas
1 shallot
½ tsp salt
Few drops of chilli sauce
2 Tbsp dried prawns
Oil for deep-frying

To garnish:
16 cooked prawns
Leaf coriander sprigs

1 Soak the peas in a bowl of cold water for 24 hours. Drain, then cover with fresh cold water and rub the peas between the palms of your hands to loosen their skins. Leave the skins to float, then skim them off with a slotted spoon and drain the peas thoroughly.

2 Peel and finely chop the shallot. Place in a food processor and add the peas, salt, chilli sauce and dried prawns. Grind to a soft, smooth purée.

3 Heat oil for deep-frying to 180°C/350°F. Drop small spoonfuls of the purée into the oil and fry for 3 to 4 minutes or until golden brown. Serve warm topped with the prawns and a small sprig of coriander.

Samosas

THESE VEGETABLE-STUFFED PASTIES FROM INDIA CAN BE SERVED HOT OR COLD. ACCOMPANY THEM WITH MANGO CHUTNEY OR A DIPPING SAUCE OF THIN NATURAL YOGHURT MIXED WITH PLENTY OF CHOPPED FRESH MINT OR A DUST OF PAPRIKA. IN INDIA COOKS WOULD FRY THE SAMOSAS IN GHEE, CLARIFIED BUTTER THAT CAN BE HEATED TO A HIGH TEMPERATURE, BUT OIL CAN BE USED.

MAKES 16

Pastry:
350 g/12 oz plain flour
Pinch of salt
6 Tbsp oil or ghee, plus extra
    for shallow and deep-frying
125 ml/4½ fl oz warm water

Filling:
450 g/1 lb potatoes
225 g/8 oz cauliflower
175 g/6 oz peas
2 shallots
2 Tbsp curry paste
2 Tbsp chopped fresh coriander
1 Tbsp lemon juice
Salt and pepper

1 To make the pastry, sift the flour and salt into a bowl. Stir in 6 tablespoons of oil or ghee, then gradually add the warm water and mix to a dough.

2 Knead the dough on a floured board until smooth, wrap in cling film and leave to rest for about 30 minutes.

3 To make the filling, scrub the potatoes and, without peeling, cook them in a pan of boiling water until tender. Drain and when cool, peel and chop into small dice.

4 Divide the cauliflower into tiny florets and blanch in a saucepan of boiling water for 2 to 3 minutes or until just tender, then drain. If using fresh peas, blanch them with the cauliflower, if using frozen they need no pre-cooking.

5 Peel and slice the shallots. Heat 3 tablespoons of oil in a large frying pan and fry the shallots until soft. Add the potatoes, cauliflower, peas, curry paste, coriander and lemon juice and cook over a low heat for 2 to 3 minutes, stirring frequently. Set aside to cool.

6 Divide the pastry into 8 and, keeping the pieces you are not working with covered, roll one piece to a 18 cm/7 in round. Cut in half and shape each semi-circle into a cone, dampening the edges to seal. Spoon in a little of the filling, dampen the top and press down over the filling to enclose it. Use the remaining pastry and filling to make 16 samosas.

7 Heat oil for deep-frying to 180°C/350°F and fry the samosas in batches for 3 to 4 minutes until golden brown on both sides. Drain and serve hot or cold.

Sesame Turkey Bites

THESE ARE GOOD SERVED WITH A CREAMY TOMATO AND RED PEPPER DIP, TOMATO SALSA OR AVOCADO AND BLUE CHEESE DIP (SEE PAGE 52). THEY CAN BE SERVED HOT OR COLD.

MAKES ABOUT 30

Turkey Bites:
450 g/1 lb minced raw turkey
    breast
1 Tbsp snipped fresh chives
2 tsp wholegrain mustard
Salt and pepper
4 Tbsp white sesame seeds
1 Tbsp black sesame seeds
Oil for deep-frying

Dip:
½ red pepper
6 Tbsp curd cheese
2 Tbsp tomato ketchup
Dash of Tabasco
2 tsp snipped fresh chives

To serve:
15 cherry tomatoes, halved
Cucumber slices or wedges

1 To make the turkey bites, mix together the minced turkey, chives, mustard and seasoning in a bowl. Roll the mixture into about 30 walnut-sized balls.

2 Mix the white and black sesame seeds together and roll the turkey balls in the seeds until coated. Chill for 30 minutes or longer.

3 Heat oil for deep-frying to 160°C/325°F and fry the turkey balls in batches for 3 to 4 minutes until golden.

4 To make the dip, finely chop the red pepper. Mix together the curd cheese, ketchup and Tabasco until smooth. Stir in the red pepper and sprinkle with the chives.

5 Drain the turkey balls and skewer on cocktail sticks with half a cherry tomato. Serve with the dip.

Pork and Prawn Wontons

SERVE THESE CRISP LITTLE 'MONEYBAGS' WITH AN ORIENTAL DIPPING SAUCE SUCH AS CHILLI, SWEET AND SOUR, PLUM OR DARK SOY. WONTON WRAPPERS ARE AVAILABLE IN PACKS FROM THE CHILLER CABINETS OF CHINESE SUPERMARKETS.

MAKES 20

150 g/5 oz raw prawns
3 canned water chestnuts
2 spring onions
200 g/7 oz lean minced pork
1 tsp finely grated fresh ginger
2 Tbsp light soy sauce
1 Tbsp oyster sauce
1 Tbsp fish sauce
20 wonton wrappers
1 egg white, lightly beaten
Oil for deep-frying

1 Peel and devein the prawns and chop finely. Finely chop the water chestnuts and spring onions. Put the pork, ginger, prawns, water chestnuts, soy, oyster and fish sauces and spring onions in bowl and stir until well mixed.

2 Place a teaspoon of the mixture in the centre of a wonton wrapper, brush the edges of the wrapper with egg white and gather it around the filling, pressing the edges together at the top to make a 'money bag' shape. As you make them, place the filled wontons on a floured board, spaced slightly apart, so they don't stick to the board or each other.

3 Heat oil for deep-frying to 170 °C/325 °F and cook in batches for 3 minutes or until golden and crisp.

4 Drain the wontons and serve hot with the dipping sauce.

Spicy Thai Fish Cakes with Coriander Soy Dip

THESE CAN BE ALSO SERVED AS AN APPETIZER WITH A SMALL SALAD GARNISH AND THE DIPPING SAUCE SPOONED OVER. A MIXTURE OF SALMON AND A FIRM WHITE FISH SUCH AS MONKFISH IS USED HERE BUT YOU COULD USE ALL SALMON IF YOU PREFER.

MAKES 20

225 g/8 oz salmon fillet,
    skinned
225 g/8 oz firm white fish fillet,
    e.g., monkfish
100 g/4 oz fine green beans
1 tsp fresh lemon grass purée
1 tsp fresh ginger purée
Finely grated zest of 1 lime
1 Tbsp fish sauce
1 Tbsp chopped fresh coriander
1 egg white, lightly beaten
Flour, to dust
Oil for deep-frying

Dip:
1 Tbsp coriander seeds
4 Tbsp dark soy sauce
1 Tbsp white wine vinegar
½ tsp sugar
A few fresh coriander leaves,
    chopped

1 Cut the salmon and white fish into chunks. Trim and finely chop the green beans.

2 Place the salmon, white fish, lemon grass purée, ginger purée and lime zest in a food processor and blend until coarsely minced – be careful not to reduce the mixture to a paste. Transfer to a bowl and stir in the fish sauce, coriander, green beans and egg white.

3 With floured hands, shape into small balls and flatten into round cakes, about 1 cm/½ in thick. Chill for 30 minutes.

4 To make the dip, toast the sesame seeds in a dry, heavy frying pan until golden. Remove from the pan and mix with the soy sauce, vinegar and sugar, stirring until the sugar dissolves. Pour into a serving bowl and float a few fresh coriander leaves on top.

5 Heat oil for deep-frying to 160 °C/325 °F. Fry in batches for 2 to 3 minutes until golden. Drain and serve with the dipping sauce.

Fried Cheese with Cranberry and Olive Relish ILLUSTRATED LEFT

USE SMALL, INDIVIDUAL PORTIONS OF CAMEMBERT OR WEDGES OF BRIE CUT FROM A LARGE CHEESE. WHICHEVER YOU USE, THE CHEESE SHOULD BE QUITE FIRM SO IT DOESN'T MELT IN THE HOT OIL.

SERVES 4

3 Tbsp plain flour
1 egg
75 g/3 oz dry breadcrumbs
8 small wedges of Camembert
    or Brie
4 Tbsp cranberry sauce
1 Tbsp chopped pitted olives
Oil for deep-frying
Salad, to garnish

1 Spread out the flour on a plate, beat the egg in a shallow dish and spoon the breadcrumbs on to another plate.

2 Dust the cheese wedges with flour, dip in the beaten egg and then press on the crumbs until well coated. Chill for 30 minutes.

3 Heat oil for deep-frying to 180°C/350°F and fry the cheeses in two batches for about 1 to 2 minutes each or until golden. Drain on kitchen paper.

4 Warm the cranberry sauce with the olives. Stir well and serve with the hot cheese. Accompany with a salad garnish.

Spinach and Feta Cigars

IF USING FROZEN SPINACH, THAW IT COMPLETELY AND THEN DRY IT OFF IN A DRY, HEAVY FRYING PAN OVER A LOW HEAT UNTIL ALL THE EXCESS MOISTURE HAS EVAPORATED.

MAKES 20

75 g/3 oz feta cheese
225 g/8 oz cooked spinach
50 g/2 oz cottage cheese
1 tsp chopped fresh mint
Pinch of ground nutmeg
10 sheets of filo pastry,
    measuring 19 x 30 cm
    (7 x 12 in)
1 egg white, lightly beaten
Oil for deep-frying

1 Crumble the feta cheese and chop the spinach. In a bowl, mix together the spinach, cottage cheese, feta, mint and nutmeg, stirring until evenly combined.

2 Cut the filo sheets in half to give 20 squares. Spoon a little of the spinach mixture down the centre of one square, brush the edges with egg white and roll up the pastry around the filling in a cigar shape, pressing the edges together to seal.

3 Repeat with the rest of the filo squares and the filling to make 20 cigars.

4 Heat oil for deep-frying to 180°C/350°F and fry the cigars in batches for 2 to 3 minutes or until golden brown. Drain and serve warm.

Cheese Aigrettes with Chilli Tomato Sauce

ADD A STRONGLY-FLAVOURED HARD CHEESE, SUCH AS PARMESAN, TO THE AIGRETTES AND VARY THE AMOUNT OF CHILLI IN THE SAUCE ACCORDING TO PERSONAL TASTE.

SERVES 4

Tomato sauce:
450 g/1 lb ripe tomatoes
2 shallots
1 small red chilli
2 Tbsp olive oil
1 tsp dried oregano
1 tsp sugar

Aigrettes:
150 ml/¼ pt cold water
50 g/2 oz butter
65 g/2½ oz plain flour
2 eggs, beaten
2 Tbsp grated hard cheese, e.g.,
    Parmesan
1 tsp mustard powder
Oil for deep-frying
Extra grated Parmesan, to dust

1 To make the tomato sauce, peel, deseed and chop the tomatoes. Peel and finely chop the shallots, deseed and finely chop the chilli.

2 Heat the olive oil in a pan, add the shallots and fry until softened. Add the chilli, tomatoes, oregano and sugar and simmer uncovered for 15 to 20 minutes so the excess liquid in the tomatoes evaporates and you have a thick sauce – mash the tomatoes occasionally so they break down.

3 To make the aigrettes, put the water in a pan, cut the butter into small pieces and add. Heat until the butter melts, then bring to a fast boil. Remove from the heat and add all the flour in one go. Beat with a wooden spoon until you have a smooth mixture that leaves the sides of the pan.

4 Gradually beat in the eggs until the paste is soft and glossy but still holds its shape. Finally beat in the cheese and mustard powder.

5 Heat oil for deep-frying to 180 °C/350 °F. Drop large spoonfuls of the mixture into the hot oil and fry for 5 minutes or until golden brown all over. Drain, dust with extra Parmesan and serve at once with the warm sauce.

2 | appetisers

Serving an appetiser that complements the dishes to follow, is one of the secrets of a successful dinner party. If your main course is rich and full flavoured, opt for a simple starter that's not too filling, if the main course is a lighter dish of chicken or fish, the starter can be more substantial. While delicious to eat, some deep-fried foods can look dull if served on their own, so add a dusting of paprika or finely grated cheese, a few scattered chives, a lettuce leaf and cherry tomato or a fresh herb sprig for a colourful garnish.

Chinese Aromatic and Crispy Duck

SIMILAR TO THE WORLD-FAMOUS PEKING DUCK BUT SIMPLER TO PREPARE. IT MAKES AN EXCELLENT STARTER FOR A CHINESE DINNER PARTY BUT COULD ALSO BE SERVED AS A MAIN COURSE FOR 2 TO 3 PEOPLE. AS THE DUCK HAS TO STEAM FOR SEVERAL HOURS AND THEN BE LEFT TO COOL, IT IS WORTH DOING THE INITIAL COOKING THE DAY BEFORE YOU PLAN TO SERVE IT.

SERVES 4 TO 6

1 plump duck, weighing about 1.6 kg/3½ lb

Marinade:
6 Tbsp light soy sauce
2 Tbsp rice wine or dry sherry
2 tsp Chinese five spice powder
2 tsp grated fresh root ginger
Oil for deep-frying

To serve:
Thin Chinese pancakes
Plum dipping sauce
Shredded spring onions
Cucumber batons

1 Remove the wing tips from the duck and split it in half lengthways (or ask the butcher to do this for you). Rinse the duck halves and pat dry with absorbent paper.

2 To make the marinade, whisk together the soy sauce, rice wine or sherry, five spice powder and ginger in a shallow dish large enough to take both halves of the duck. Place the duck in the dish and baste it with the marinade. Cover and leave in a cool place for 3 to 4 hours, turning the duck over from time to time.

3 Transfer the duck to a steamer (add any remaining marinade to the steaming water) and steam for 3 hours, topping up the water as necessary.

4 Remove the duck from the steamer and leave overnight in a cool, dry place. It is important for the duck skin to be dry or it will not crisp when fried.

5 Heat oil for deep-frying to 180°C/350°F and deep-fry the duck halves, skin side down, for 5 to 6 minutes or until deep golden brown and crisp. Drain the duck and shred the meat and skin into small pieces.

6 To serve, spread the pancakes with plum sauce and top with pieces of duck, shredded spring onions and cucumber batons, roll up and eat.

Pumpkin Puffs with Avocado and Blue Cheese Dip

IF MAKING THE DIP MORE THAN 1 HOUR BEFORE SERVING, PRESS A PIECE OF CLING FILM OVER THE SURFACE TO EXCLUDE THE AIR AND PREVENT THE AVOCADO TURNING BROWN.

SERVES 4

450 g/1 lb pumpkin (peeled and
    deseeded weight)
4 spring onions
1 Tbsp butter
Salt and pepper
1 egg, beaten
2 Tbsp plain flour
Oil for deep-frying

Avocado and blue cheese dip:
1 ripe avocado
1 Tbsp lemon juice
50 g/2 oz crumbled blue cheese
150 ml/¼ pt Greek-style natural
    yoghurt
Few drops of Tabasco sauce

1 Cut the pumpkin into chunks and steam for 10 minutes or until tender. Drain and mash. Finely chop the spring onions and stir into the mashed pumpkin with the butter, seasoning, beaten egg and flour.

2 Heat oil for deep-frying to 180°C/350°F. Using a large spoon, drop spoonfuls of the pumpkin mix into the hot oil and fry in batches for 3 to 4 minutes until golden brown.

3 To make the dip, peel and mash the avocado with the lemon juice. Mix in the blue cheese, yoghurt and Tabasco sauce to taste. Alternatively, the ingredients can be puréed together in a food processor.

4 Serve the hot fritters with the dip.

Walnut Chicken

SERVE AS A DINNER PARTY APPETISER WITH THE CORIANDER AND CARROT PURÉE OR AS PART OF A FINGER FOOD BUFFET WITH A LEMON OR CURRY MAYONNAISE DIP.

SERVES 6

4 chicken breasts, skinned and
   boned
Juice of 1 lemon
1 tsp grated fresh root ginger
Flour, to dust
1 egg, beaten
150 g/5 oz finely chopped
   walnuts
Oil for deep-frying

Coriander and carrot purée:
450 g/1 lb carrots
300 ml/½ pt chicken stock
2 Tbsp chopped fresh coriander

1 Cut each chicken breast across into 4 or 5 strips. Spread out in a shallow dish and add the lemon juice and ginger. Allow to marinate for several hours, turning the chicken occasionally.

2 Lift the chicken pieces from the marinade and pat dry with absorbent paper. Dust them with flour, brush with beaten egg and press on the chopped walnuts until evenly coated. Chill for 30 minutes or until ready to cook.

3 Heat oil for deep-frying to 180°C/350°F and fry the chicken in batches for 3 to 4 minutes until cooked through and the coating is a rich golden brown.

4 To make the purée, peel and chop the carrots and simmer in the stock in a covered pan for 10 minutes or until tender. Purée the carrots and cooking liquid and stir in the coriander. Serve warm with the chicken.

Suppli di Riso

CRISP-COATED BALLS OF RISOTTO RICE ARE POPULAR ALL OVER ITALY AND ARE MADE WITH A VARIETY OF FILLINGS INCLUDING MEAT, CHEESE OR VEGETABLES.

SERVES 4

175 g/6 oz risotto (arborio) rice
Salt and pepper
1 egg, beaten
150 g/5 oz mozzarella cheese
150 g/5 oz dry breadcrumbs
½ tsp dried marjoram
Oil for deep-frying

To serve:
Chunky tomato pasta sauce

1 Cook the rice in a pan of boiling water for 12 to 15 minutes until just tender, or according to the packet instructions. Drain and leave to cool. Then, season the rice with salt and pepper and stir in the beaten egg.

2 Cut the mozzarella into 12 cubes. Place a tablespoon of rice in one hand, add a cube of cheese and cover the cheese with more rice. Mould the rice around the cheese and press into a ball. Repeat with the remaining rice and cheese.

3 Mix together the breadcrumbs and marjoram. Roll the rice balls in the crumb mixture until coated. Chill for 2 to 3 hours.

4 Heat oil for deep-frying to 190°C/375°F and fry the balls in 2 or 3 batches for 3 to 4 minutes until golden. Drain and serve hot with chunky tomato sauce.

Lobster and Avocado Cups

EITHER CHINESE SPRING ROLL WRAPPERS OR FILO PASTRY CAN BE USED TO MAKE THE 'CUPS' AND CUT THE SHEETS TO THE CORRECT SIZE WITH SCISSORS IF NECESSARY. FOR CONVENIENCE, THE CUPS CAN BE PREPARED AND FRIED SEVERAL HOURS AHEAD AND KING PRAWNS, CRAYFISH OR A MIX OF DIFFERENT SEAFOOD CAN REPLACE THE LOBSTER IN THE FILLING.

SERVES 4

12 squares of filo pastry or
    spring roll wrappers,
    roughly 18 cm/7 in in size
Oil for deep-frying
450 g/1 lb cooked lobster meat
1 avocado
Juice of 1 lime
4 cherry tomatoes
¼ cucumber
½ bag of mixed lettuce leaves
4 Tbsp seafood or Thousand
    Island dressing
4 tsp lumpfish caviar or salmon
    roe

1 Layer up the filo squares or spring roll wrappers in stacks of three, dampening each sheet to help the layers stick together and positioning the corners at different angles. Cover with a sheet of plastic wrap and a damp cloth to prevent the pastry drying out.

2 Heat oil for deep-frying to 180°C/350°F. Carefully add one stack of pastry to the oil, place a ladle in the centre and press down into a cup shape. Fry for 3 to 4 minutes until golden brown, using the ladle to ensure the pastry 'cup' keeps its shape and stays immersed in the oil but avoid pressing down too firmly or the pastry will stick firmly to the ladle, making it difficult to remove without breaking.

3 Remove from the oil and gently loosen the cup from the ladle. Fry three more cups in the same way and leave to cool.

4 Cut the lobster meat into bite-sized pieces. Peel and slice the avocado and toss with the lime juice. Halve the cherry tomatoes and slice the cucumber.

5 Place the cups on serving plates and line with lettuce leaves. Fill with the lobster, avocado, tomatoes and cucumber. Spoon on the dressing and roe.

Prawn Wraps with a Lemon Grass Dip

IT'S IMPORTANT TO USE GREEN (RAW) PRAWNS AS READY-COOKED ONES WILL OVERCOOK IN THE HOT OIL AND LOSE THEIR FLAVOUR AND SUCCULENCE.

SERVES 4

Dip:
1 stick of lemon grass or 1 tsp
    lemon grass purée
1 red chilli
1 tsp light brown sugar
4 Tbsp soy sauce
1 Tbsp rice vinegar
1 Tbsp chopped fresh coriander

Prawns:
12 large green tiger prawns
12 pieces of filo pastry or
    Chinese spring roll
    wrappers, each measuring
    18 x 7.5 cm/7 x 3 in
1 egg, beaten
Oil for deep-frying

1 For the dip, if using a stick of lemon grass, chop into very fine pieces. Deseed and finely chop the chilli. Mix together the lemon grass, chilli, sugar, soy sauce and vinegar and set aside for 1 hour for the flavours to infuse. When ready to serve, pour into a bowl or divide between four small dishes and scatter over the coriander.

2 For the prawns, peel off the shells and remove the heads but leave the tails on. Slit down the back of each prawn and pull out the black thread running down it. Rinse the prawns and pat dry with kitchen paper.

3 Place one piece of filo or spring roll wrapper on a board. Brush the edges with beaten egg, place a prawn at one end and roll the wrapper around it, leaving the prawn tail exposed. Press the wrapper edges together to seal. Repeat with the remaining prawns and wrappers.

4 Put the wrapped prawns side by side on a plate and chill until ready to cook. Heat oil for deep-frying to 180°C/350°F and fry the prawns in batches for 2 minutes or until golden brown.

5 Drain and serve hot with the dip. Garnish with lime wedges.

Miso Soup with Fried Bean Curd

DASHI IS A LIGHT STOCK WIDELY USED IN JAPANESE CUISINE. PACKS OF READY-MADE DASHI ARE AVAILABLE FROM JAPANESE FOOD STORES BUT DETAILS OF HOW TO PREPARE IT ARE GIVEN HERE IF YOU PREFER TO MAKE YOUR OWN. KELP, BONITO FLAKES AND MISO CAN ALSO BE FOUND IN JAPANESE GROCERS.

SERVES 4

Dashi stock:
1 cm/½ in strip of dried kelp
1.2 litres/2 pt water
2 Tbsp dried bonito flakes

Other ingredients:
75 g/3 oz shiitake mushrooms
½ red pepper
200 g/7 oz firm tofu (beancurd)
50 g/2 oz mangetout
50 g/2 oz brown or red miso
Flour, to dust
Oil for deep-frying

1 Wipe the kelp with a damp cloth and cut into three or four pieces. Place the pieces in a large saucepan with the water and bring slowly to the boil. As the water comes up to the boil, remove the kelp with a draining spoon and discard.

2 Sprinkle in the bonito flakes and remove the pan from the heat. As soon as the flakes start to sink, strain the stock through a fine sieve and discard the flakes.

3 When ready to make the soup, slice the mushrooms and red pepper, cut the tofu into small cubes and slice the mangetout.

4 Heat the dashi stock in a pan until simmering. Add the miso and stir until dissolved. Add the mushrooms and mangetout and leave the soup over a low heat, without letting it boil, while you cook the tofu.

5 Dust the cubes of tofu with flour and heat oil for deep-frying to 180°C/350°F. Fry the tofu for 1 to 2 minutes until golden, drain and divide between four bowls. Ladle the soup into the bowls and serve at once.

Salmon Beignets with Creamy Fennel Sauce

FENNEL'S MILD ANISEED FLAVOUR GOES VERY WELL WITH FISH AND THESE LIGHT, CRISP BEIGNETS MAKE A DELICIOUS STARTER. THEY COULD ALSO BE SERVED AS A STYLISH SUPPER DISH, WASHED DOWN WITH A CRISP GLASS OF CALIFORNIAN CHARDONNAY.

SERVES 6

75 g/3 oz butter
150 ml/¼ pt water
75 ml/3 fl oz milk
100 g/4 oz strong plain flour
3 medium eggs, beaten
150 g/5 oz hot smoked salmon,
    cooked
2 Tbsp grated Parmesan
½ tsp paprika
1 Tbsp lemon juice
Salt and pepper
Oil for deep-frying

Sauce:
6 Tbsp lemon mayonnaise
4 Tbsp soured cream
1 Tbsp finely chopped fresh
    fennel sprigs

1 Cut up the butter into small pieces and place in a saucepan with the water and milk. Heat until the butter melts, bring to a rolling boil and add the flour in one go. Beat with a wooden spoon until the mixture forms a smooth ball.

2 Allow to cool slightly, then beat in the eggs a little at a time until you have a soft mixture that holds its shape.

3 Remove any skin and bones from the salmon and flake the flesh. Stir into the batter with the Parmesan, paprika, lemon juice and seasoning.

4 Heat oil for deep-frying to 170°C/325°F and drop in walnut-sized balls of the mixture. Fry in batches for 5 to 6 minutes or until golden.

5 To make the sauce, stir the mayonnaise, soured cream and fennel together until combined. Drain the beignets and serve hot with the sauce.

Crisp-fried Avocado Rings with Prawn Sauce

A VARIATION ON THE TRADITIONAL AVOCADO WITH PRAWNS, THIS MAKES AN UNUSUAL DINNER PARTY APPETISER. IT'S IMPORTANT THE AVOCADOS ARE RIPE BUT IF THEY ARE OVER-RIPE THEY WILL BE DIFFICULT TO COAT WITH THE CRUMBS. THE RINGS SHOULD BE FRIED WITHIN 30 MINUTES OF COATING THEM TO AVOID DISCOLOURATION.

SERVES 4

75 g/3 oz of fresh breadcrumbs,
    white or brown
1 Tbsp ground hazelnuts
2 large avocados
Flour, to dust
1 egg, beaten
Oil for deep-frying

Sauce:
100 g/4 oz peeled prawns
2 Tbsp tomato ketchup
2 Tbsp mayonnaise
4 Tbsp single cream
Juice of 1 lime

To garnish:
4 whole prawns
4 lime wedges
2 tablespoons chopped parsley
¼ teaspoon paprika

1 Mix together the breadcrumbs and hazelnuts and spread out on a plate.

2 Cut the unpeeled avocados into rings about 5 mm/¼ in thick using a small sharp knife and gently ease the rings off the stones. Peel away the skin from the rings, dip them in flour, brush with beaten egg and coat with the crumb mixture.

3 Heat about 2.5 cm/1 in oil in a large frying-pan to 180°C/350°F and fry the avocado rings for 2 to 3 minutes until golden, turning over after 1 minute. Drain.

4 To make the sauce, coarsely chop the prawns and mix with the ketchup, mayonnaise, single cream and lime juice. Serve with the warm avocado rings and garnish with whole prawns, lime wedges, chopped parsley and a sprinkling of paprika.

Halloumi and Courgette Fritters

HALLOUMI IS A FIRM, WHITE CHEESE FROM CYPRUS AND HAS A TANGY, SALTY TASTE. IT CAN BE FOUND IN LARGER SUPERMARKETS AND GREEK FOOD SHOPS.

SERVES 4

150 g/5 oz halloumi cheese
100 g/4 oz feta cheese
1 courgette
75 g/3 oz plain flour
2 Tbsp milk
1 large egg
2 Tbsp chopped fresh coriander
 or parsley
Oil for deep-frying
4 Tbsp Greek yoghurt
½ tsp paprika

1 Cut the halloumi cheese into fine dice, crumble the feta and grate the courgette.

2 In a bowl, mix together the halloumi, feta, courgette and flour. Whisk together the milk and egg and stir into the cheese mixture with half the coriander or parsley to make a thick batter.

3 Heat oil for deep-frying to 180°C/350°F. Using a large spoon, drop three spoonfuls of the mixture into the oil and fry for 30 seconds on each side or until golden brown.

4 Drain and fry the remaining mixture in the same way to make 12 fritters.

5 Divide the warm fritters between serving plates and spoon the yoghurt alongside. Dust with the paprika and scatter over the remaining coriander or parsley.

Cauliflower Cheese Bites

SERVE AS AN APPETISER WITH A SPOONFUL OF THOUSAND ISLAND DRESSING AND A SMALL SALAD GARNISH, OR AS A VEGETABLE ACCOMPANIMENT TO SAUSAGES, BURGERS OR PLAINLY GRILLED MEAT.

SERVES 4

1 medium size cauliflower
100 g/4 oz plain flour
Pinch of mustard powder
Salt and pepper
2 eggs, separated
75 g/3 oz grated Cheddar
 cheese
2 Tbsp oil, plus extra for deep-
 frying
100 ml/4 fl oz water
Flour, to dust

1 Divide the cauliflower into small florets, discarding the tough centre stalk. Cook the florets in a pan of boiling water for about 5 minutes or until just tender. Drain.

2 Sift the flour and mustard into a bowl and season with pepper. Stir in the egg yolks, cheese, 2 tablespoons of oil and the water, whisking until you have a smooth batter.

3 Heat oil for deep-frying to 190°C/375°F. While the oil is heating up, whisk the egg whites until stiff and fold into the batter.

4 Dust the cauliflower florets with flour and dip them into the batter until they are well coated. Deep-fry for about 4 minutes until golden brown, drain and serve at once.

3 | meat & poultry

The Chinese are famous for their deep-fried meat dishes such as Sweet and Sour Pork and Lemon Chicken, while the Ukraine introduced gourmets to Chicken Kiev, but it is the United States that has turned its Southern Fried Chicken into one of the world's most popular fast foods. These are just a few of the tasty fried foods featured in this chapter.

Southern Fried Chicken with Cream Gravy

THERE ARE ALMOST AS MANY WAYS OF COOKING THIS FAMOUS DISH AS THERE ARE SOUTHERN STATES, ONE OF THE MOST POPULAR COMING FROM MARYLAND (SEE PAGE 30). THIS VERSION COATS THE CHICKEN IN A MIX OF HERBS AND CAJUN SPICES.

SERVES 4

8 chicken joints, a mix of
   drumsticks and thighs
225 g/8 oz plain flour
Salt and pepper
1 tsp mixed dried herbs
1 tsp Cajun seasoning
1 tsp caster sugar
Oil for deep-frying

Cream gravy:
2 Tbsp plain flour
225 ml/8 fl oz full-fat milk

1 Rinse the chicken joints and pat dry with kitchen paper.

2 Put the flour, salt, pepper, herbs, Cajun seasoning and caster sugar in a plastic food bag, seal the top and shake well to combine. Add the chicken pieces, two at a time, and toss to coat with the flour mixture. Place the coated chicken pieces on a plate and chill for 30 minutes.

3 Heat oil for deep-frying to 170°C/325°F and fry the chicken for about 15 minutes until golden brown. Drain and test the chicken is cooked through, either by cutting into the flesh with a sharp knife or by using a meat thermometer.

4 To make the cream gravy, spoon 2 tablespoons of the frying oil into a saucepan and stir in the flour. Cook for 1 minute, then remove from the heat and gradually mix in the milk. Return to a low heat and stir until thickened and smooth.

5 Serve the chicken with the gravy and accompany with vegetables of your choice.

Gingered Lemon Chicken

A CANTONESE DISH FROM HONG KONG THAT CAN BE SERVED WITH EGG-FRIED RICE, PLAIN BOILED RICE OR EGG NOODLES. AS THE VEGETABLES ARE STIR-FRIED FIRST, BEFORE EXTRA OIL IS ADDED TO DEEP-FRY THE CHICKEN, A WOK IS THE MOST PRACTICAL PAN TO USE.

SERVES 4

1 quantity of Simple Flour and Water Batter (see page 14)
1 red pepper
1 courgette
4 spring onions
4 boneless chicken breasts, skinned
2 Tbsp oil, plus extra for deep-frying
Flour for dusting

Lemon sauce:
1½ Tbsp cornflour
100 ml/4 fl oz freshly-squeezed lemon juice
350 ml/12 fl oz chicken stock
2 Tbsp clear honey
2 Tbsp light brown sugar
1 Tbsp grated root ginger

1 Make up the batter and leave to stand for at least 30 minutes.

2 Deseed and chop the red pepper, slice or chop the courgette and chop the spring onions. Cut each chicken breast into 3 pieces.

3 Heat 2 tablespoons of oil in a wok and stir-fry the pepper, courgette and spring onions for 3 to 4 minutes until starting to soften. Remove from the pan and keep warm in a low oven.

4 Add extra oil to the wok to deep-fry the chicken and heat to 180°C/350°F. Dip the chicken pieces in flour and then in the batter and deep-fry for 8 to 10 minutes until golden.

5 For the sauce, whisk the cornflour and lemon juice together until smooth. Pour into a saucepan and stir in the stock, honey, sugar and root ginger. Stir over a low heat until the sauce comes to the boil and it clears and thickens. Simmer for 1 minute.

6 Drain the chicken and serve with the vegetables with the lemon sauce spooned over.

Rice Vermicelli with Chicken and Prawns

IN THE FAR EAST, COOKS USE WOKS FOR DEEP-FRYING AS WELL AS STIR-FRYING AND THIS RECIPE IS A COMBINATION OF BOTH COOKING METHODS.

SERVES 4

1 Tbsp lime juice
1 tsp crushed garlic
1 Tbsp brown sugar
3 Tbsp light soy sauce
1 Tbsp rice vinegar
250 g/9 oz boneless chicken
    breasts
1 carrot
1 red pepper
1 small courgette
200 g/7 oz rice vermicelli
Oil for deep-frying
175 g/6 oz peeled prawns
2 eggs, beaten
2 Tbsp chopped fresh coriander

1 Whisk together the lime juice, garlic, sugar, soy sauce and vinegar. Set to one side.

2 Skin the chicken breasts and cut the flesh into thin strips. Peel and cut the carrot into matchsticks, deseed and chop the red pepper and cut the courgette into matchsticks.

3 Snip the dry vermicelli into short lengths and soak in warm water for a few minutes until softened. Spread out on a tray and leave until dry.

4 Heat oil for deep-frying in a wok to 190 °C/375 °F and fry the vermicelli in batches until light golden and crisp. Drain and set aside.

5 Pour off most of the oil from the wok, leaving about 2 tablespoons. Reheat, add the chicken and stir-fry for 3 minutes. Remove and set aside. Add the carrot, red pepper and courgette and stir-fry for 3 minutes.

6 Return the chicken to the wok, add the prawns and pour in the soy sauce mixture. Toss over the heat for 1 to 2 minutes, add the beaten eggs and stir until they have set. Add the vermicelli and toss together until well mixed.

7 Serve at once before the noodles have started to soften, with the coriander sprinkled over.

Chicken Kiev

IN THIS RECIPE IT IS ESSENTIAL THE OIL IS HEATED TO THE CORRECT TEMPERATURE. IF IT IS TOO HOT, THE CRUMB COATING WILL BROWN TOO QUICKLY BEFORE THE CHICKEN INSIDE IS COOKED. SHOULD THIS HAPPEN, DRAIN THE CHICKEN JOINTS, PLACE THEM ON A BAKING SHEET AND FINISH COOKING IN A 180°C/350°F FOR 10 TO 15 MINUTES.

SERVES 4

4 large garlic cloves

Salt and pepper

4 Tbsp chopped fresh parsley

75 g/3 oz butter, at room temperature

1 tsp lemon juice

4 x 225 g/8 oz chicken supremes (breasts with wing bones attached), skinned

Flour, to dust

3 eggs, beaten

225 g/8 oz dry breadcrumbs

Light olive oil for deep-frying

1 Crush the garlic on a board with a little salt and mix with the parsley. Work in the butter and lemon juice and season with pepper. Spoon the mixture on to a sheet of cling film and shape into a log approximately 1 cm/½ in thick. Wrap the film around the butter and twist the ends in a tight parcel. Chill or freeze until firm.

2 Place each supreme between two sheets of cling film and beat with a rolling pin or the flat side of a meat mallet, avoiding the wing bone. The supremes should be beaten out to roughly double their size and the thinner the edges are, the better the 'seal' will be.

3 Unwrap the garlic butter and cut into four sticks. Open up the breast part of each supreme and place a butter stick in the centre. Wrap the flesh around the butter, tucking in the sides to enclose it completely.

4 Dust each supreme with flour, brush with beaten egg and coat in breadcrumbs. Chill for 1 hour and then coat with a second layer of flour, egg and crumbs. Chill for 2 hours or until ready to cook.

5 Heat the oil to 180°C/350°F and deep-fry the supremes in two batches for 10 minutes, carefully turning them over halfway. Drain and serve with new potatoes and a green vegetable such as broccoli or peas.

Mushroom and Parmesan Chicken

A VARIATION ON CHICKEN KIEV, IN THIS RECIPE THE CHICKEN IS STUFFED WITH MUSHROOMS AND PARSLEY RATHER THAN GARLIC BUTTER. USE OPEN MUSHROOMS WITH DARK GILLS SO THE FILLING CONTRASTS WELL WITH THE PALE FLESH OF THE CHICKEN AND COOK THEM UNTIL ANY EXCESS LIQUID HAS EVAPORATED.

SERVES 4

2 spring onions
1 garlic clove
100 g/4 oz mushrooms
1 Tbsp butter
3 Tbsp chopped fresh parsley
4 chicken breasts, skinned and boned
Flour, to dust
2 eggs, beaten
75 g/3 oz fresh breadcrumbs
2 Tbsp grated Parmesan cheese
Oil for deep-frying

1 Trim and thinly slice the spring onions. Peel and crush the garlic and finely chop the mushrooms.

2 Heat the butter in a pan and fry the onions for 1 minute. Stir in the garlic and mushrooms and cook for 2 minutes. Increase the heat under the pan slightly and continue to cook until the mushroom mixture is quite dry. Stir in 1 tablespoon of the parsley and set aside to cool.

3 Cut a pocket in each chicken breast and fill with the mushroom mixture. Reshape the breasts so the filling is enclosed by the meat.

4 Coat the chicken in flour and brush with beaten egg. Mix together the breadcrumbs, Parmesan and remaining parsley and press over the chicken until evenly covered. Chill for at least 30 minutes before cooking.

5 Heat oil for deep-frying to 180°C/350°F and fry the chicken for 10 minutes, turning the breasts over once. Drain and serve with mixed vegetables.

Turkey Croquettes with Pineapple and Redcurrant Sauce

A FRUIT SAUCE, SUCH AS THIS ONE MADE WITH PINEAPPLE JUICE AND REDCURRANTS, PROVIDES A TANGY CONTRAST TO A MILDY-FLAVOURED MEAT LIKE TURKEY. IF PREFERRED, CRANBERRIES COULD BE USED INSTEAD OF REDCURRANTS OR SIMPLY SERVE THE CROQUETTES WITH TOMATO CHUTNEY OR KETCHUP.

SERVES 4

Croquettes:
6 spring onions
75 g/3 oz butter
90 g/3½ oz plain flour, plus extra to dust
300 ml/½ pt milk
2 egg yolks
50 g/2 oz grated Cheddar cheese
350 g/12 oz cooked turkey breast, minced
175 g/6 oz sweetcorn kernels
Salt and pepper
5 Tbsp dry breadcrumbs
1 Tbsp grated Parmesan
1 egg, beaten

Sauce:
5 Tbsp unsweetened pineapple juice
250 g/9 oz fresh or frozen redcurrants
75 g/3 oz soft light brown sugar
Oil for deep-frying

1 Trim the spring onions and chop finely. Heat the butter in a pan and fry the onions until softened. Remove the pan from the heat, blend in the flour and stir in the milk.

2 Return the pan to a low heat and bring to the boil, stirring until smooth and thickened. Simmer for 1 minute, remove from the heat and beat in the egg yolks and cheese. Stir in the minced turkey and sweetcorn kernels, season with salt and pepper and leave to cool.

3 Transfer the mixture to a bowl, cover and chill for 1 hour.

4 Mix together the dry breadcrumbs and Parmesan. Divide the turkey mixture into 8 equal portions and shape into croquettes. Dust them with flour, brush with beaten egg and coat in the crumbs and Parmesan. Chill again until ready to cook.

5 To make the sauce, simmer the pineapple juice, redcurrants and sugar together in a pan for 10 minutes or until the currants are soft, mashing occasionally with a fork.

6 Heat oil for deep-frying to 180°C/350°F and deep-fry the croquettes in two batches for 3 to 4 minutes until golden brown.

Herby Sausage and Apple Patties

SERVE THESE TASTY PATTIES WITH MASHED POTATOES AND GRILLED TOMATOES OR A
MIXED SALAD.

SERVES 4

1 medium onion
1 dessert apple
450 g/1 lb pork sausage meat
1 Tbsp chopped fresh sage
1 Tbsp Dijon mustard
Salt and pepper
Flour, for dusting
1 egg, beaten
75 g/3 oz dry breadcrumbs
Oil for deep-frying

1 Peel and finely chop the onion. Peel, core and finely chop or grate the apple.

2 In a bowl, mix together the sausage meat, onion, apple, sage and mustard. Season to taste.

3 With damp hands, shape the mixture into 12 small flat patties. Dust the patties with flour, brush with beaten egg and press over the dry crumbs until each one is well coated. Place them on a plate in a single layer and chill for 1 hour.

4 Heat oil for deep-frying to 180°C/350°F and fry the patties for 6 to 7 minutes until cooked through. Drain and serve hot.

Pork with Orange and Tarragon Sauce

MATZO MEAL MAKES A CRISP, CRUNCHY COATING FOR MEAT AND FISH BUT DRY BREADCRUMBS
COULD BE USED INSTEAD.

SERVES 4

100 g/4 oz matzo meal
1 tsp mixed dried herbs
Flour, to dust
8 thin pork steaks, total weight
    about 700 g/1½ lb
1 egg, beaten
Oil for deep-frying

Sauce:
150 g/5 oz button mushrooms
50 g/2 oz butter
2 Tbsp cornflour
300 ml/½ pt chicken stock
Juice of ½ orange
1 tsp Dijon mustard
100 ml/4 fl oz single cream
2 Tbsp chopped fresh tarragon
Salt and pepper

1 Mix together the matzo meal and dried herbs. Dust the pork steaks with flour, brush with beaten egg and press over the matzo meal to cover completely.

2 Heat oil for deep-frying to 180°C/350°F and fry the crumbed steaks in two batches for 4 to 5 minutes until golden brown and cooked through, turning over once. Drain and keep warm in a low oven while you make the sauce.

3 Quarter or slice the mushrooms. Melt the butter in a saucepan and fry the mushrooms for 2 to 3 minutes. Stir in the cornflour off the heat, then blend in the chicken stock, orange juice and mustard. Return to a low heat and stir until smooth and thickened. Simmer for 1 minute before stirring in the cream and tarragon.

4 Season the sauce with salt and pepper and serve spooned over the pork. Accompany with seasonal vegetables.

Turkey Cordon Bleu

THIS RECIPE CAN ALSO BE MADE WITH CHICKEN BREASTS, FOLLOWING THE METHOD GIVEN FOR THE
CHICKEN KIEV RECIPE ON PAGE 68, BUT SUBSTITUTING THE HAM AND CHEESE SLICES FOR THE GARLIC
BUTTER. SERVE WITH TOMATO AND MASCARPONE SAUCE OR ANOTHER TOMATO-BASED SAUCE.

SERVES 4

8 thin turkey steaks or turkey
   breast slices
4 thin slices of ham
4 thin slices of Gruyère cheese
75 g/3 oz fresh breadcrumbs
1 Tbsp snipped fresh chives
Flour, to dust
1 egg, beaten
Oil for deep-frying

Sauce:
300 ml/½ pt tomato pasta sauce
100 g/4 oz mascarpone cheese
1 Tbsp snipped fresh chives

1 Lay the turkey between two sheets of cling film and beat out
using a rolling pin or the flat side of a meat mallet until it is
quite thin.

2 Place four of the steaks on a board, top each one with a slice
of ham and cheese and cover the filling by pressing the
remaining steaks on top.

3 Mix together the breadcrumbs and chives and spread out on
a plate. Dust the turkey with flour, brush with beaten egg
and coat with the crumb mix. Chill for 1 hour.

4 Heat about 2.5 cm/1 in oil to 170°C/335°F in a deep frying
pan and fry the turkey parcels, two at a time, for 8 to 10
minutes until golden brown, turning over half way.

5 Whilst the turkey is cooking, gently warm the sauce
ingredients without letting them boil, and stirring until the
mascarpone is evenly blended in. Drain the turkey and serve
with the sauce.

Cantonese Sweet and Sour Pork

A FAVOURITE DISH IN CANTONESE RESTAURANTS AROUND THE WORLD. THE CHINESE WOULD USE BELLY PORK BUT THIS RECIPE USES LEAN STEAKS CUT FROM THE SHOULDER OR LEG. A WOK CAN BE USED TO COOK THE PORK AND THE VEGETABLES BUT, IF YOU PREFER, STIR-FRY THE VEGETABLES IN A LARGE FRYING PAN.

SERVES 4

1 quantity of Beer Batter No 1 (see page 14)

Sweet and sour sauce:
100 ml/4 fl oz chicken stock
3 Tbsp rice vinegar
1 Tbsp clear honey
3 Tbsp light soy sauce
2 Tbsp tomato ketchup
1 tsp cornflour

Pork:
45 g/1 lb pork steaks
Oil for deep-frying
Flour, to dust
1 garlic clove
1 yellow or orange pepper
8 spring onions
8 lychees
4 Tbsp unsalted cashew nuts
1 tsp fresh ginger purée

1 Make up the batter and leave to stand for at least 30 minutes.

2 To make the sauce, place all the ingredients except the cornflour in a saucepan and heat gently. Mix the cornflour with 1 tablespoon of water, add to the pan and stir continuously until the sauce is smooth and thickened. Simmer for 1 minute, then remove from the heat and set aside.

3 To cook the pork, cut the meat into 2-cm/¾-in pieces. Heat oil in a wok or deep-fat fryer to 180°C/350°F. Dust the pork in flour, coat in the batter and deep-fry for 3 to 4 minutes until golden brown and crisp. Drain and keep the pork warm in a low oven.

4 If using a wok, carefully pour off all but 2 tablespoons of the oil. If using a fryer, spoon off the same quantity of oil into a large frying pan.

5 Peel and finely chop the garlic, deseed and chop the pepper, trim and cut the spring onions into 2.5-cm/1-in lengths. Peel the lychees and remove the stones.

6 Heat the oil in the wok or frying pan and add the cashews. Stir-fry for 30 seconds until golden, then drain. Add the garlic, pepper and ginger to the pan and stir-fry for 3 minutes. Add the spring onions and lychees, stir-fry for 1 minute, and then add the pork.

7 Pour in the sauce, toss the ingredients together until coated and simmer for 2 minutes. Scatter over the cashews and serve immediately with fried or boiled rice and crispy seaweed (see page 102).

Mixed Leaf Salad with Garlic Croutons and Parma Ham

A DELICIOUSLY CRUNCHY SALAD THAT HAS PLENTY OF STRONG FLAVOURS. CHOOSE A CRUMBLY BLUE CHEESE SUCH AS ROQUEFORT OR STILTON AND A MIX OF DIFFERENT SALAD LEAVES – COS LETTUCE, ROCKET AND FRISÉE ALL WORK WELL.

SERVES 4

2 large slices of thick-sliced
    sour dough or another
    country bread
4 slices of Parma ham
2 garlic cloves
2 sticks of celery
½ green pepper
225 g/8 oz mixed salad leaves,
    e.g., Cos lettuce, wild rocket,
    frisée or iceberg lettuce
175 g/6 oz blue cheese, e.g.,
    Stilton or Roquefort
50 g/2 oz walnut pieces
Oil for deep-frying

Dressing:
6 Tbsp extra virgin olive oil
2 Tbsp balsamic vinegar
Salt and pepper

1 Remove the crusts from the bread and cut into 1 cm/½ in dice. Tear or cut the Parma ham into 2.5 cm/1 in strips. Peel the garlic, slice the celery and chop the green pepper.

2 Wash and dry the salad leaves and tear larger ones into bite-sized pieces. Cube or crumble the blue cheese and scatter over the leaves with the celery, green pepper and walnuts.

3 Heat 2.5 cm/1 in oil in a large frying pan, add the garlic and fry until the cloves turn golden brown. Fish them out with a slotted spoon and continue heating the oil until it reaches 180°C/350°F.

4 Fry the bread cubes for 2 minutes or until golden, then drain. Add the strips of Parma ham to the oil and fry for 1 to 2 minutes until crisp. Drain.

5 To make the dressing, whisk the olive oil, vinegar and seasoning together and drizzle over the salad. Scatter over the croutons and crisp ham and serve.

Crispy Duck Rolls

SIMMERING THE DUCK BREASTS ENSURES THE MEAT STAYS TENDER AND SUCCULENT, WHEREAS IT CAN DRY OUT UNDER A GRILL. RESERVE THE COOKING LIQUID AND ONCE COLD, CHILL IT SO THE FAT SOLIDIFIES ON THE SURFACE. THIS CAN BE LIFTED OFF AND USED FOR FRYING POTATOES, WHILST THE STOCK CAN BE STORED IN THE FREEZER FOR ANOTHER RECIPE.

SERVES 4

3 small or 2 large duck breasts
2 bay leaves
8 black peppercorns
1 large onion
1 red pepper
100 g/4 oz shiitake mushrooms
Oil for shallow and deep-frying
1 tsp grated root ginger
100 g/4 oz cucumber
3 Tbsp hoi sin sauce
1 Tbsp rice vinegar
12 spring roll wrappers
1 egg, beaten

1 Place the duck breasts in a pan with the bay leaves and peppercorns and pour over cold water to cover. Bring to the boil, cover the pan, lower the heat and simmer gently for 1 hour. Leave the duck to cool in the liquid, then drain, discard the skin and chop the meat.

2 Peel and finely slice the onion, deseed and chop the pepper and chop or slice the mushrooms. Heat 2 tablespoons of oil in a frying pan, add the onion and cook gently until softened. Add the pepper, mushrooms and ginger and fry for a further 5 minutes. Transfer to a bowl and leave to cool.

3 Cut the cucumber into small dice and add to the vegetables in the bowl with the duck, hoi sin sauce and rice vinegar, stirring until mixed.

4 Place a spring roll wrapper on a board and top with a tablespoon of the duck mixture. Brush the edges of the wrapper with the egg and roll up around the filling, tucking in the sides and pressing the edges together to seal. Repeat with the remaining wrappers and filling.

5 Heat oil to 180°C/350°F and deep-fry the rolls for 3 to 4 minutes until golden brown and crisp. Drain and serve hot with extra hoi sin sauce for dipping.

Lamb Pooris

GOLDEN CUSHIONS OF CRISP DOUGH BASED ON THE INDIAN BREAD CALLED POORI AND FILLED
WITH A RICH MIX OF LAMB AND VEGETABLES.

MAKES 20

Dough:
65 g/2½ oz butter
225 g/8 oz plain flour
Water to mix

Filling:
1 carrot
1 small parsnip
4 spring onions
2 Tbsp oil, plus extra for deep-
    frying
225 g/8 oz lean minced lamb
1 Tbsp curry paste
2 Tbsp tomato purée
225 ml/8 fl oz lamb stock

1 To make the dough, cut up the butter into small pieces and rub into the flour. Add enough cold water to mix to a soft dough, about 100 ml/4 fl oz. Knead the dough until smooth on a lightly floured surface, then cover with cling film and chill for 30 minutes.

2 To make the filling, peel and cut the carrot and parsnip into small pieces. Cook in a pan of boiling water for 5 minutes or until just tender. Drain.

3 Trim and chop the spring onions. Heat 2 tablespoons of oil in a frying pan and fry the onions for 2 minutes until soft. Add the minced lamb and fry until it browns, breaking up any clumps of meat with a spoon.

4 Add the carrot and parsnip and stir in the curry paste and tomato purée. Pour in the stock, bring to the boil and simmer for 15 minutes until the liquid has evaporated, stirring occasionally so the meat doesn't stick to the pan. Allow to cool.

5 Roll out the dough thinly on a floured surface. Using a plain cutter, stamp out twenty 10-cm/4-in rounds, gathering and re-rolling the dough trimmings as necessary. Dampen the edges of the rounds with water and spoon a little of the meat mixture on each. Fold the dough over the filling and press the edges firmly together to seal.

6 Heat oil for deep-frying to 180°C/350°F and deep-fry the pooris in batches for 3 to 4 minutes or until golden brown. Drain and serve with mango chutney and a tomato and cucumber salad.

Sesame Lamb in Potato Nests

IF YOU HAVE A WOK, USE IT TO DEEP-FRY THE POTATO NESTS AND THEN CAREFULLY POUR OFF THE
EXCESS OIL BEFORE USING THE WOK TO STIR-FRY THE LAMB. IF NOT, FRY THE NESTS IN A LARGE
SAUCEPAN OR DEEP-FAT FRYER AND USE A FRYING PAN TO COOK THE LAMB. THE NESTS CAN BE
KEPT WARM ON A RACK IN A LOW OVEN WHILE THE LAMB COOKS.

SERVES 2

Potato nests:
225 g/8 oz potatoes
4 tsp cornflour
Oil for deep-frying

Sesame lamb:
½ red pepper
1 small courgette
4 baby corn
350 g/12 oz lean lamb
2 Tbsp hoi sin sauce
1 Tbsp dark soy sauce
2 tsp sesame oil
1 Tbsp sesame seeds

1 Peel the potatoes, coarsely grate into strips and toss with
the cornflour until coated. Line a metal sieve (around
15 cm/6 in across) with half the potato strips and place
another sieve or ladle on top to hold the potato in place.

2 Heat oil in a wok for deep-frying to 180 °C/350 °F, lower in
the sieves and fry for 2 to 3 minutes or until the potato is
golden brown. Remove the sieves from the oil and carefully
lift out the potato basket. Drain and keep warm while you
cook the second basket.

3 To cook the lamb, deseed and slice the pepper, cut the
courgette into matchsticks and halve the corn lengthways.
Trim any fat from the lamb and cut into strips.

4 Carefully pour all but 2 tablespoons of the oil out of the
wok and stir-fry the pepper, courgette and corn for 3 to
4 minutes. Remove from the pan and keep warm. Add
the lamb to the wok and stir-fry over a brisk heat for 2 to
3 minutes. Pour in the hoi sin sauce and soy sauce, toss
until the lamb is coated and drizzle over the sesame oil.

5 Return the vegetables to the wok, stir-fry for 1 to 2 minutes
and then scatter over the sesame seeds. Transfer the potato
baskets to serving plates and pile in the stir-fried lamb and
vegetables. Serve at once.

Noodle Baskets with Black Bean Beef

THE BASKETS CAN BE MADE UP TO TWO DAYS IN ADVANCE, STORED IN AN AIRTIGHT CONTAINER IN THE REFRIGERATOR AND THEN REHEATED IN A MODERATE OVEN WHEN NEEDED. REMEMBER TO USE METAL STRAINERS FOR FRYING THE BASKETS AS PLASTIC ONES WILL MELT IN THE HOT OIL.

SERVES 4

225 g/8 oz thin egg noodles
Oil for deep-frying, plus 2 Tbsp
    and extra for greasing

Black bean beef:
350 g/12 oz sirloin or fillet
    steak, trimmed of fat
1 stick of celery
½ yellow or orange pepper
4 cherry tomatoes
6 Tbsp Chinese black bean stir-
    fry sauce

1 Plunge the noodles into a saucepan of boiling water for 4 minutes until tender (or according to the packet instructions). Drain and rinse by running cold water through the sieve. Spread out the noodles on a tray and leave to dry.

2 Lightly oil a metal strainer, measuring roughly 12 cm/5 in in diameter, and line it with one quarter of the noodles. Press down in an even layer. Oil the base of a slightly smaller strainer and press down lightly on top of the noodles.

3 Heat oil for deep-frying to 190°C/375°F in a wok or other wide, deep pan. Hold the handles of the strainers together (protect your hand with an oven glove) and lower the strainers into the oil. Cook for about 3 minutes or until the noodles are crisp and golden.

4 Remove the strainers from the oil and carefully lift out the top one. Run a knife around the noodle basket to loosen it, turn the strainer over and tap carefully to release the basket. Make three more baskets in the same way.

5 For the beef, cut the steak into thin strips, slice the celery and pepper and halve the tomatoes. Heat 2 tablespoons of oil in a wok or large frying pan and stir-fry the steak over a high heat for 2 to 3 minutes.

6 Remove the beef from the pan, add the celery and pepper and stir-fry for 3 minutes. Add the cherry tomato halves and stir-fry for 1 minute. Return the beef to the pan, pour in the black bean sauce and toss the meat and vegetables together until coated with the sauce and piping hot. Spoon into the baskets and serve.

4 | fish & shellfish

As fish and shellfish have such delicate flesh, it is especially important to give them a protective coating before deep-frying. The coating not only prevents the fish over-cooking and drying out during frying but also helps to trap any juices inside the flesh, keeping it moist and stopping the juices from leaking out and tainting the oil. Breadcrumbs, batter, polenta or oatmeal all make good coatings for fish and shellfish and these can be flavoured with herbs, spices or citrus zest.

Lemon and Herb Sardines ILLUSTRATED RIGHT

ASK THE FISHMONGER TO SCALE, CLEAN AND REMOVE THE SARDINES HEADS. SPLIT THE FISH OPEN ALONG THE UNDERSIDE, LAY THEM SKIN SIDE UP ON A BOARD AND PRESS YOUR THUMBS DOWN THE BACK TO LOOSEN THE BONES, SNIPPING THE BACKBONE JUST ABOVE THE TAIL WITH SCISSORS. TURN THEM OVER AND GENTLY PULL AWAY THE BACK AND RIB BONES IN ONE STEP.

SERVES 4

12 sardines, split open and
    filleted
Flour, to dust
1 egg
2 Tbsp milk
175 g/6 oz fresh breadcrumbs
1 Tbsp finely chopped tarragon
1 Tbsp finely chopped fresh
    parsley
Oil for deep-frying

To serve:
Lemon wedges

1 Dust the sardines with flour. Beat the egg and milk together in a shallow dish. Mix the breadcrumbs with the parsley and tarragon and spread out on a plate.

2 Dip the sardines in the egg and milk mixture and coat well with the crumbs.

3 Heat oil for deep-frying to 180°C/350°F and fry the sardines in batches for 2 to 3 minutes or until golden. Drain and serve at once with wedges of lemon to squeeze over.

Herrings in Oatmeal

OATMEAL MAKES A LIGHT CRISP COATING IN THIS TRADITIONAL SCOTTISH DISH. THE COATING CAN ALSO BE USED FOR OTHER FIRM FISH FILLETS SUCH AS SOLE, MACKEREL OR COD.

SERVES 2

2 herrings, filleted
3 Tbsp plain flour
¼ tsp mustard powder
Pinch of salt
6 Tbsp medium oatmeal
1 tsp dried thyme
1 egg, beaten
Oil for deep-frying
Lemon wedges, to serve

1 Rinse the herring fillets and pat dry with absorbent kitchen paper. Mix together the flour, mustard and salt. On a separate plate, mix together the oatmeal and thyme.

2 Coat the herrings in the flour mix, dip in the beaten egg and coat with the oatmeal, pressing it firmly over the fish. Chill for 30 minutes or until ready to cook.

3 Heat oil for deep-frying to 180°C/350°F and fry the herring fillets, two at a time, for 3 to 4 minutes until golden brown, turning over half way.

4 Drain and serve with lemon wedges to squeeze over. Accompany with new potatoes and peas.

Traditional English Fried Fish ILLUSTRATED LEFT

YEAST BATTER WORKS PARTICULARLY WELL WITH FRIED FISH AS IT STAYS CRISP TO THE LAST BITE!

SERVES 4

700 g/1½ lb firm white fish
    fillets, e.g., cod or haddock
Salt and pepper
Flour, for coating
1 quantity of yeast batter (see
    page 14)
Oil for deep-frying

To garnish:
Fried parsley (see page 111)
Lemon wedges
English-style 'chip shop' chips
    (see page 119)

1 Skin the fish fillets and cut into four equal portions. Season with salt and pepper.

2 Dust the fillets with flour and then dip in the batter until well coated.

3 Heat oil for deep-frying to 190 °C/375 °F. Fry the fish in the hot oil, two fillets at a time, for about 5 minutes or until golden brown. Drain and keep warm.

4 Serve the fish garnished with the deep-fried parsley sprigs and lemon wedges. Accompany with chips.

Pecan-crusted Sole Goujons

FRESH BREADCRUMBS CAN BE MADE WHENEVER YOU HAVE LEFT-OVER BREAD. REDUCE THE BREAD TO CRUMBS IN A FOOD PROCESSOR (WITH OR WITHOUT CRUSTS), AND FREEZE IN TIGHTLY SEALED BAGS. MARK THE WEIGHT OF CRUMBS ON THE OUTSIDE OF THE BAG UNTIL NEEDED.

SERVES 4

75 g/3 oz fresh breadcrumbs
2 Tbsp finely chopped pecans
2 Tbsp finely grated hard
    cheese, e.g., Cheddar
Salt and pepper
550 g/1¼ lb sole fillets, cut into
    7.5 cm/3 in strips
Flour, for dusting
4 Tbsp mayonnaise
2 Tbsp chopped fresh tarragon
Oil for deep-frying
Lemon wedges, to serve

1 Mix together the breadcrumbs, chopped pecans and grated cheese and spread out on a large plate. Season the strips of fish and dust lightly with flour.

2 In a shallow dish, mix together the mayonnaise and tarragon. Add the fish and stir until coated.

3 Lift out the pieces of sole and toss in the crumbs. Spread out on a plate and chill for 30 minutes.

4 Deep-fry the sole in oil heated to 180 °C/350 °F for 2 to 3 minutes until golden brown. Drain and serve hot, garnished with lemon wedges.

Devilled Whitebait with Gremolata

GREMOLATA IS A TANGY MIX OF PARSLEY, GARLIC AND LEMON ZEST THAT THE ITALIANS SPRINKLE OVER FULL-FLAVOURED MEAT DISHES LIKE OSSOBUCO. IT ALSO WORKS WELL WITH FISH.

SERVES 4

Gremolata:
Finely grated zest of 1 lemon
3 Tbsp finely chopped flat-leaf
    parsley
2 garlic cloves, finely chopped

Whitebait:
100 g/4 oz plain flour
½ tsp hot chilli powder
Salt and pepper
700 g/1½ lb whitebait
Oil for deep-frying

1 For the gremolata, mix the lemon zest, parsley and garlic together in a small dish.

2 For the whitebait, put the flour, chilli powder and salt and pepper to taste in a large plastic food bag. Rinse the whitebait in a colander, pat dry and add to the bag. Shake quite vigorously so the whitebait are coated with the flour.

3 Heat oil for deep-frying to 190°C/375°F. Deep-fry the whitebait in three or four batches for about 3 minutes each until the fish are crisp and lightly golden.

4 Drain and serve sprinkled with the gremolata.

ILLUSTRATED RIGHT

Fritto Misto

FRIED FISH ITALIAN STYLE, THIS IS A PARTICULARLY POPULAR DISH ALONG THE COAST OF NAPLES WHERE LOCAL CATCHES ENSURE AN ABUNDANCE OF SEAFOOD.

SERVES 4

225 g/8 oz self-raising flour,
    plus extra for dusting
½ tsp bicarbonate of soda
Salt and pepper
300 ml/½ pt water
900 g/2 lb mixed seafood, e.g.,
    large prawns, baby squid,
    white fish fillets
Oil for deep-frying

To serve:
2 anchovy fillets, chopped
1 Tbsp chopped capers
1 Tbsp chopped baby gherkins
8 Tbsp mayonnaise

1 Sift the flour and bicarbonate of soda into a bowl and season with salt and pepper. Make a well in the centre, pour in half the water and stir until mixed. Gradually stir in the rest of the water to make a smooth batter.

2 Prepare the seafood by peeling the prawns (leave the tails on) and cutting the fish fillets into small pieces.

3 Heat oil for deep-frying to 180°C/350°F. Dust the prepared seafood in flour, dip in the batter and fry in the hot oil for 2 to 3 minutes until golden brown.

4 To serve, chop the anchovies, capers and gherkins and stir into the mayonnaise. Drain the seafood and serve at once with the mayonnaise.

Salt and Pepper Squid

BEFORE FRYING THE SQUID, SCORE THE FLESH WITH A SHARP KNIFE IN A LATTICE PATTERN SO THE PIECES CURL ATTRACTIVELY AS THEY COOK. TAKE CARE NOT TO CUT TOO DEEPLY, HOWEVER, AS THE FLESH IS DELICATE AND YOU COULD END UP SHREDDING IT!

SERVES 4

Dressing:
½ tsp sweet chilli sauce
½ tsp crushed garlic
1 tsp brown sugar
Juice of 2 limes
6 Tbsp Thai fish sauce

Squid:
2 tsp freshly ground white
    pepper
1 tsp salt
100 g/4 oz plain flour
2 garlic cloves
Oil for deep-frying
500 g/1 lb 2 oz (cleaned weight)
    medium sized squid, scored
2 Tbsp chopped fresh coriander

1 For the dressing, whisk together the chilli sauce, garlic, brown sugar, lime juice and fish sauce.

2 For the squid, mix the pepper, salt and flour together in a bowl. Peel the garlic cloves and leave whole.

3 Heat oil for deep-frying to 180°C/350°F. Toss the squid in the seasoned flour until it is well coated and add about a quarter to the hot oil. Fry for 4 to 5 minutes until the squid curls and becomes crisp. Drain and keep warm in a low oven whilst you fry the remainder in three batches.

4 Divide the squid between serving plates and scatter over the coriander. Drizzle the dressing around the squid.

5 Serve at once with a little salt sprinkled over, accompanied with lemon wedges.

Gingered Crab Cakes

VARY THE AMOUNT OF CHILLI ACCORDING TO PERSONAL TASTE – ADD MORE IF YOU WANT THE CRAB CAKES TO HAVE A REAL KICK, LESS IF YOU DON'T WANT THEM TOO HOT.

SERVES 4

550 g/1¼ lb potatoes
Salt and pepper
4 spring onions
1 red or green chilli
8 anchovy fillets
1½ tsp crushed garlic
1 tsp grated root ginger
Finely grated zest of 1 lime
2 Tbsp chopped fresh coriander
2 Tbsp snipped fresh chives
400 g/14 oz white crab meat
Plain flour, for dusting
2 eggs, beaten
75 g/3 oz fresh breadcrumbs
Oil for deep-frying

1 Peel the potatoes, cut into even-size pieces and cook in a pan of boiling, salted water until tender. Drain, mash and leave to cool.

2 Chop the spring onions, deseed and finely chop the chilli and snip the anchovies into small pieces with scissors. Stir the onions, chilli and anchovies into the potatoes with the garlic, ginger, lime zest, coriander, chives and crab meat. Season to taste with salt and pepper.

3 Shape the mixture into 12 balls, place on a plate and chill for 30 minutes. Dust the crab cakes with flour, brush with beaten egg and coat in the breadcrumbs.

4 Deep fry in hot oil at 170°C/335°F for 7 to 8 minutes until golden brown. Drain and serve at once with tartare sauce or lemon mayonnaise.

Tempura Prawns in Barbecue Sauce

SMALL CHUNKS OF FIRM WHITE FISH CAN ALSO BE COOKED USING THE SAME METHOD
DEMONSTRATED BELOW. IF USING FROZEN PRAWNS, DEFROST THEM THOROUGHLY AND
PAT DRY WITH KITCHEN PAPER BEFORE COATING THEM IN THE BATTER AND COOKING.

SERVES 4

16 large raw prawns
1 red pepper
1 green pepper
Oil for deep-frying
1 quantity of Tempura Batter
   (see page 14)

Barbecue sauce:
1 Tbsp sweet chilli sauce
2 Tbsp light soy sauce
1 Tbsp sugar
2 Tbsp rice vinegar
4 Tbsp tomato ketchup
225 ml/8 fl oz chicken stock
1 Tbsp cornflour

1 Shell the prawns, removing the heads but leaving the tails on if preferred. Cut down the back of each prawn and pull out the black thread running down it. Rinse the prawns and pat dry with kitchen paper.

2 Deseed and slice the red and green peppers.

3 Heat oil for deep-frying to 180°C/350°F. Dip the prawns and pepper slices in the batter and deep-fry in batches in the hot oil for 3 to 4 minutes or until golden and crisp.

4 To make the barbecue sauce, mix the chilli sauce, soy sauce, sugar, vinegar, ketchup and stock together in a pan. Blend the cornflour with 3 tablespoons water until smooth, add to the pan and bring to the boil over a low heat, stirring constantly. Simmer for 1 minute.

5 Drain the prawns and peppers and serve with the sauce spooned over. Accompany with egg noodles.

Spiced Squid Rings with Jalapeno Salsa

MARINATE THE SQUID RINGS FOR SEVERAL HOURS BEFORE COOKING TO HELP TENDERISE THEM AND ADD EXTRA FLAVOUR.

SERVES 4

450 g/1 lb cleaned squid, cut
    into rings
2 large garlic cloves
3 Tbsp olive oil
3 Tbsp lemon juice
1 tsp paprika
Flour, to dust
2 tsp curry paste
1 quantity of Yeast Batter or
    Beer Batter No 2 (see page
    14)
Oil for deep-frying

Salsa:
1 red onion
2 medium tomatoes
1 fresh or bottled green
    jalapeno pepper
2 garlic cloves
1 Tbsp chopped fresh parsley
Salt and pepper
4 Tbsp olive oil
1 Tbsp white wine vinegar

1 Put the squid in a bowl. Peel and crush the garlic and mix with the olive oil, lemon juice and paprika. Pour over the squid, stir until the rings are coated and leave to marinate for 3 to 4 hours.

2 Drain the squid and dust with flour. Stir the curry paste into the batter.

3 Heat oil for deep-frying to 180°C/350°F. Coat the squid rings in the batter and deep-fry for about 2 minutes or until golden and crisp. Drain.

4 To make the salsa, peel and finely chop the onion. Chop the tomatoes, deseed and finely chop the jalapeno pepper, peel and finely chop the garlic. Mix the onion, tomatoes, pepper, garlic and parsley together and season with salt and pepper. Whisk the olive oil and vinegar together and pour over.

5 Pile the squid rings on serving plates and serve with the salsa.

Mussel Fritters with Tartare Sauce

SERVE THESE AS A LIGHT MEAL WITH THE SAUCE IN A SMALL DISH ALONGSIDE. GARNISH EACH
PLATE WITH A COUPLE OF SPOONFULS OF QUARTERED CHERRY TOMATOES MIXED WITH CHOPPED
RADISHES AND CUCUMBER.

SERVES 4

20 large mussels, e.g., Green Lip
Flour, to dust
Oil for deep-frying
1 quantity of Beer Batter No 1
 (see page 14)

Tartare sauce:
6 Tbsp mayonnaise
1 Tbsp finely chopped gherkins
2 tsp chopped capers
1 Tbsp chopped fresh parsley

1 Rinse the mussels and pat dry with absorbent paper. Dust lightly with flour.

2 Heat oil for deep-frying to 180°C/350°F. Dip the mussels in the batter and fry in the oil for 2 to 3 minutes or until golden brown and crisp.

3 To make the sauce, mix together the mayonnaise, gherkins, capers and parsley and spoon into individual dishes.

4 Drain the mussels and serve hot with the Tartare Sauce. Accompany with cherry tomato salad.

ILLUSTRATED RIGHT

Monkfish with Gingered Hoi Sin Sauce

HOI SIN IS A CHINESE SAUCE USED FOR GLAZING SPARE RIBS AND CHICKEN WINGS AND IT MAKES
AN EXCELLENT DIP FOR SPRING ROLLS.

SERVES 4

550 g/1¼ lb monkfish fillet
Flour, to dust
1 red onion
1 red pepper
2 garlic cloves
50 g/2 oz mangetout
Oil for stir-frying and deep-
 frying
1 quantity of Simple Flour and
 Water Batter (see page 14)
1 tsp fresh ginger purée
6 Tbsp hoi sin sauce
2 Tbsp rice vinegar
2 Tbsp light soy sauce

1 Cut the monkfish into 4-cm/1½-in pieces and dust with flour.

2 Peel and slice the onion, deseed and chop the pepper, peel and finely chop the garlic and slice the mangetout lengthways into three or four strips.

3 Heat 2 tablespoons of oil in a frying pan, add the onion, pepper and ginger and stir-fry for 3 minutes. Add the mangetout and garlic and stir-fry for 2 minutes. Stir in the hoi sin sauce, rice vinegar and soy sauce and leave to simmer over a gentle heat while you cook the fish.

4 Heat oil for deep-frying to 180°C/350°F. Stir the batter and add half the fish pieces to it. Lift them out one by one, add to the hot oil and fry for 3 to 4 minutes until they are crisp. Drain and fry the remaining fish in the same way.

5 Serve the sauce and vegetables spooned over the fish and accompany with boiled or egg-fried rice.

Tuna, Prawn and Potato Cakes with Avocado Salsa

TUNA WORKS WELL IN THIS RECIPE AS IT HAS A FIRM, DENSE TEXTURE BUT OTHER FISH SUCH AS MONKFISH, SOLE OR SALMON COULD ALSO BE USED.

SERVES 4

250 g/9 oz fresh tuna fillet
400 g/14 oz potatoes
50 g/2 oz butter
1 Tbsp chopped fresh dill
2 egg yolks
Salt and pepper
16 cooked prawns, peeled
Flour, to dust
2 eggs, beaten
75 g/3 oz fresh breadcrumbs
Oil for deep-frying

Salsa:
1 avocado
2 tomatoes
Juice of 1 lime
1 Tbsp olive oil
Dash of Tabasco

1 Grill or pan-fry the tuna for about 5 minutes or until just cooked through. Leave to cool, then remove any skin and finely flake or chop the flesh.

2 Peel the potatoes, cut into chunks and cook in a pan of boiling water until tender. Drain and mash with the butter. Add the dill and egg yolks, season with salt and pepper and stir in the tuna.

3 Leave to cool and then shape the mixture into 16 oval cakes. Press a prawn into the centre of each, covering the prawn completely. Dust the cakes with flour, brush with beaten egg and coat in the breadcrumbs. Chill for 1 hour.

4 Heat oil for deep-frying to 180°C/350°F and fry the cakes in batches for 5 minutes or until crisp and golden. Drain.

5 To make the salsa, halve the avocado, remove the stone, peel and chop the flesh. Skin, deseed and chop the tomatoes and mix with the avocado, lime juice, olive oil and Tabasco. Serve the salsa with the hot tuna and potato cakes.

5 | vegetables

Deep-fried vegetables are a popular part of most cuisines, turning up as pakoras in India, fried seaweed in China, sweetcorn cakes in Thailand or tempura in Japan. The vegetables are usually cut into small pieces before being coated in batter, crumbs or choux paste, so only need frying for a short time to become deliciously light and crisp on the outside but still retain a little 'bite' in the middle.

180°

190°

Crisp and Crunchy Onion Rings

LARGE SWEET ONIONS WORK BEST FOR THIS RECIPE. THE RINGS CAN BE SERVED ON THEIR OWN, WITH A MUSTARD, SPICY TOMATO OR SOUR CREAM DIP, OR AS A GARNISH FOR BURGERS, STEAKS AND MEATLOAF.

SERVES 4

1 large white onion
Flour, to dust
1 egg white
150 g/5 oz matzo meal or fine
    cornmeal
½ tsp ground cumin
Oil for deep-frying

1 Peel the onion and cut into 5-mm/¼-in slices. Separate each slice into individual rings.

2 Dust the rings with flour. Lightly beat the egg white. Mix the matzo meal or cornmeal with the cumin and spread out on a plate.

3 Dip the onion rings in the egg white and then coat in the matzo meal.

4 Heat oil for deep-frying to 180°C/350°F and fry the onion rings in batches for 1 to 2 minutes or until crisp and golden. Drain and serve hot.

Autumn Vegetable Beignets

SERVE THESE AS A STARTER OR LIGHT MEAL AND VARY THE MIXTURE OF VEGETABLES ACCORDING TO WHAT YOU HAVE AVAILABLE.

SERVES 4

700 g/1½ lb mixed autumn
    vegetables, e.g., swede,
    carrot, parsnip, squash
Oil for roasting and deep-frying
250 g/9 oz cooked beetroot
1 tsp mixed dried herbs
1 quantity of Beer Batter No 2
    (see page 14)

1 Prepare the mixed vegetables by peeling and deseeding as necessary. Cut into two-bite size pieces.

2 Preheat the oven to 200°C/400°F. Spread out the vegetables in a shallow roasting tin, drizzle with 2 or 3 tablespoons of oil and turn until coated. Roast for 30 minutes or until the vegetables are tender. Leave to cool.

3 Peel the beetroot and cut into wedges.

4 Heat oil for deep-frying to 190°C/375°F. Stir the dried herbs into the batter and add the roasted vegetables, mixing until coated. Deep-fry in batches for 1 to 2 minutes until golden. Drain and keep warm. When all the vegetables have been fried, dip the beetroot in the batter and fry for 1 to 2 minutes.

5 Serve at once with mustard mayonnaise.

ILLUSTRATED: Crisp and Crunchy Onion Rings

Chinese Crispy 'Seaweed'

IN CHINA, COOKS WOULD MAKE THIS DISH WITH SEAWEED BUT UNFORTUNATELY THE TYPE THEY USE IS NOT YET AVAILABLE IN THE WEST. HOWEVER, SPRING GREENS, BOK CHOY OR SPINACH LEAVES CAN ALL BE SUBSTITUTED AND WORK EQUALLY WELL. STAND WELL BACK WHEN YOU ADD THE SHREDDED LEAVES TO THE HOT OIL AS MOISTURE IN THE LEAVES WILL CAUSE IT TO SPIT. SERVE THE 'SEAWEED' AS PART OF A CHINESE MEAL.

SERVES 4

2 garlic cloves
250 g/9 oz green cabbage or
    spinach leaves
Oil for deep to frying
1 tsp salt
1 tsp sugar

1 Skin the garlic and cut the cloves into wafer thin slices. Remove any tough stalks from the cabbage or spinach leaves and rinse well in cold water. Drain and dry thoroughly with kitchen paper.

2 Roll up the leaves tightly, one or two at a time, and slice very thinly with a sharp knife, about 3 mm/⅛ in thick.

3 Heat oil for deep-frying to 180°C/350°F and deep-fry the shredded greens, a handful at a time, for about 30 seconds until they turn dark green and crisp. Drain each batch before you fry the next.

4 Add the garlic with the last batch of greens, drain and toss with the rest of the fried leaves. Sprinkle with the salt and sugar and serve.

Split Pea Fritters with Roasted Red Pepper Sauce

SERVE THIS FOR AN APPETISER OR AS PART OF A VEGETARIAN MEAL. THE SPLIT PEAS NEED TO BE SOAKED OVERNIGHT SO THEY CAN BE GROUND TO A MEAL IN A FOOD PROCESSOR.

SERVES 4

Red pepper sauce:
2 large red peppers
1 Tbsp sun-dried tomato purée
about 350 g/12 fl oz vegetable
    stock

Fritters:
225 g/8 oz yellow split peas
1 small red onion
1 large garlic clove
1 Tbsp plain wholemeal flour
2 Tbsp chopped fresh coriander
½ tsp ground turmeric
½ tsp ground cumin
1 tsp baking powder
Salt and pepper
Oil for deep-frying

To garnish:
Deep-fried basil leaves

1 For the sauce, line a grill pan with foil. Place the peppers on it and grill them on all sides until their skins are scorched and black. Wrap the foil around the peppers and fold over the edges to make a tightly-sealed parcel. Leave until cool enough to handle, then unwrap the peppers, remove the stalks and seeds and strip off the skins.

2 Place the skinned peppers in a food processor with the tomato purée and half the stock. Blend to a purée, adding enough of the remaining stock to make a smooth sauce (the amount of stock needed will depend on the size of your peppers). Keep the sauce in a covered bowl in the refrigerator until needed.

3 Place the split peas in a bowl, cover with cold water and leave to soak overnight. Drain and grind the peas to a fine meal in a food processor. Peel and very finely chop the onion and crush the garlic.

4 Transfer the split pea meal to a bowl and stir in the onion, garlic, flour, coriander, turmeric, cumin, baking powder and seasoning. Beat the mixture with a wooden spoon until light and fluffy.

5 With damp hands, roll the mixture into small balls. Heat oil for deep-frying to 180°C/350°F and fry in several batches for 4 to 5 minutes until golden brown.

6 Drain, warm the red pepper sauce and serve with the hot fritters.

Felafel ILLUSTRATED LEFT

THESE CAN BE SERVED AS NIBBLES AT A PARTY OR AS A VEGETARIAN SNACK, PILED INTO PITTA BREAD WITH SALAD. IF SERVING AS NIBBLES, ACCOMPANY WITH HUMMUS OR A YOGHURT AND MINT DIP.

SERVES 4

1 red onion
2 large garlic cloves
Salt and pepper
2 x 400-g/14-oz cans of
    chickpeas, drained
2 tsp ground coriander
1 tsp ground cumin
1 tsp paprika
2 Tbsp chopped fresh parsley
1 egg, beaten
Flour, for dusting
Oil for deep-frying

1 Peel the onion and chop finely. Peel the garlic and crush with a little salt.

2 Grind the chickpeas to a meal in a food processor or mash in a bowl. Stir in the onion, garlic, coriander, cumin, paprika and parsley and season with pepper. Mix in the beaten egg until evenly combined.

3 Roll the mixture into 12 oval-shaped balls, dust with flour and flatten slightly. Chill for 1 hour.

4 Heat oil for deep-frying to 180°C/350°F and fry the falafel four at a time for 3 to 4 minutes until golden. Drain and serve warm.

Quesadillas

THESE CHEESE-FILLED TURNOVERS ARE A POPULAR SNACK IN MEXICO. USE A MIX OF TWO CONTRASTING CHEESES.

MAKES 8

½ red pepper
½ green pepper
200 g/7 oz grated mature
    Cheddar cheese
200 g/7 oz crumbled feta cheese
    or firm goat's cheese
1 tsp smoked paprika
2 Tbsp chopped fresh coriander
8 wheatflour tortillas, about
    15 cm/6 in in diameter
1 egg, beaten
Oil for deep-frying

1 Grill the pepper skins until they scorch and blacken, wrap in foil until cool enough to handle then strip away the skins. Chop the peppers into small dice.

2 In a bowl, mix together the peppers, Cheddar, feta, paprika and coriander. Divide the mixture between the tortillas, brush the edges with beaten egg and fold in half to enclose the filling, pressing the edges together to seal.

3 Heat about 2.5 cm/1 in of oil in a large deep frying pan to 180°C/350°F and fry the quesadillas for 2 to 3 minutes on each side until crisp and golden brown. Drain and serve hot with a green salad.

Indian Pakoras with Coriander Raita

INDIAN COOKS WOULD MAKE THESE FRITTERS WITH BESAN (CHICK PEA FLOUR) BUT IF YOU HAVE PROBLEMS TRACKING IT DOWN, PLAIN WHOLEMEAL FLOUR COULD BE SUBSTITUTED. USE A MIX OF DIFFERENT VEGETABLES AND PREPARE THEM AS NECESSARY. FIRMER ONES SUCH AS CAULIFLOWER FLORETS, POTATOES AND CARROTS NEED TO BE BLANCHED UNTIL THEY ARE JUST TENDER, WHILE SOFTER ONES SUCH AS AUBERGINES AND COURGETTES CAN SIMPLY BE CUT INTO CHUNKS. GARAM MASALA IS A SPICE MIX AVAILABLE FROM LARGER SUPERMARKETS AND INDIAN GROCERY STORES.

SERVES 4

225 g/8 oz besan (chick pea
    flour) or plain wholemeal
    flour
½ tsp salt
1 tsp garam masala
1 tsp ground coriander
1 tsp cumin seeds
½ tsp chilli powder
About 450 ml/16 fl oz cold water
2 egg whites
900 g/2 lb mixed vegetables,
    e.g., cauliflower florets,
    aubergines, potatoes, baby
    carrots, broccoli florets,
    courgettes
Flour, for dusting
Oil for deep-frying

Raita:
6 Tbsp thick natural yoghurt
2 Tbsp chopped fresh coriander
½ tsp black mustard seeds

1   Mix the flour, salt, garam masala, coriander, cumin seeds and chilli powder in a bowl. Add enough water to mix to a smooth batter that has the consistency of unwhipped double cream.

2   Leave the batter to stand for 1 hour or until ready to cook.

3   Whisk the egg whites until standing in soft peaks and fold into the batter. Cut the vegetables into bite-size pieces.

4   Heat oil for deep-frying to 190°C/375°F. Dust the vegetables in flour and coat in the batter, one piece at a time so they don't clump together, and fry in the hot oil for about 3 minutes until crisp and golden brown.

5   To make the raita, mix the yoghurt and coriander together and sprinkle with the mustard seeds. Drain the vegetables and serve hot with the raita.

Crispy Noodles with Chinese Vegetables

THIS RECIPE IS A GOOD WAY OF USING UP ANY LEFTOVER COOKED NOODLES. DRIED EGG NOODLES COULD ALSO BE USED BUT THEY WILL NEED TO BE COOKED FIRST.

SERVES 4

Oil for deep-frying
250 g/8 oz cooked egg noodles
700 g/1½ lb mixed vegetables,
    e.g., peppers, mangetout,
    baby corn, courgettes,
    mushrooms
1 Tbsp sunflower oil
1 Tbsp sesame oil
1 Tbsp lemon juice
2 Tbsp light soy sauce
2 Tbsp oyster sauce

1 Heat oil for deep-frying to 190 °C/375 °F – make sure you heat the oil to the correct temperature or the cooked noodles will be tough and chewy rather than crisp.

2 Cut the noodles into short lengths and deep-fry in batches for 2 to 3 minutes until golden and crisp. Drain and keep warm in the oven.

3 Prepare the vegetables as necessary and cut into bite-size pieces. Heat the sunflower and sesame oils in a wok or large frying pan and stir-fry the vegetables for 6 to 8 minutes until they start to soften.

4 Mix together the lemon juice, soy sauce and oyster sauce and pour over the vegetables. Stir-fry for another minute, tossing the vegetables so they are coated with the sauce. Serve piled on top of the crisp noodles.

Melanzane in Carrozza

AUBERGINE SLICES LAYERED WITH MOZZARELLA, DIPPED IN BATTER AND DEEP-FRIED UNTIL CRISP MAKE AN UNUSUAL LIGHT LUNCH. ACCOMPANY WITH A TANGY TOMATO AND BASIL SALAD.

SERVES 2

1 large aubergine
Freshly ground black pepper
Olive oil for brushing
6 slices of mozzarella
Flour, to dust
1 tsp Italian-style dried mixed
    herbs
1 quantity of Beer Batter No 2
    (see page 14)
Oil for deep-frying

1 Cut the aubergine into 12 thin slices, season them with pepper and brush with olive oil. Sear in a heavy ridged grill pan until just tender.

2 Leave the aubergine slices to cool. Sandwich the mozzarella between the aubergine slices and dust with flour. Stir the herbs into the batter.

3 Heat oil for deep-frying to 180 °C/350 °F, dip the mozzarella sandwiches in the batter until evenly coated and fry for 2 minutes, turning over after 1 minute, until golden and crisp on both sides. Drain and serve hot with a tomato and basil salad.

Aubergine Fritters with Aubergine Paté

AUBERGINE PATÉS ARE POPULAR IN THE MIDDLE EAST WHERE THE AUBERGINES ARE COOKED OVER A NAKED FLAME TO GIVE THEM A SMOKY, CHARGRILLED FLAVOUR. IN THIS RECIPE THEY ARE BAKED IN A CONVENTIONAL OVEN BUT THEY COULD ALSO BE COOKED ON A BARBECUE.

SERVES 4

Paté:
2 medium aubergines
1 slice of bread
2 garlic cloves
1 Tbsp lemon juice
1 Tbsp chopped fresh parsley
4 Tbsp extra virgin olive oil
Salt and pepper

Fritters:
1 large aubergine
2 Tbsp plain flour
1 quantity of Beer Batter No 1
    (see page 14)
Oil for deep-frying

1 For the paté, preheat the oven to 200°C/400°F. Score the aubergines round the centre with a sharp knife and place them on a lightly greased baking sheet. Cook in the oven for about 40 minutes or until tender.

2 Cut the aubergines in half and scoop out the flesh with a spoon. Soak the bread in a little water for 5 minutes. Skin and roughly chop the garlic. Squeeze out the bread and place in a food processor with the aubergine flesh, garlic, lemon juice, parsley and olive oil.

3 Blend together until smooth and creamy and season with salt and pepper to taste.

4 For the fritters, top and tail the aubergine and cut into 5-mm/¼-in slices. Dust with the flour. Heat oil for deep-frying to 180°C/350°F.

5 Dip the aubergine slices in the batter and deep fry in batches, 3 or 4 at a time, for 1 to 2 minutes on each side or until golden brown and crisp. Drain and keep warm in a low oven until all the slices have been cooked.

6 Serve with the aubergine paté (gently reheated in a small pan or in the microwave, if necessary) and accompany with roasted vine tomatoes.

Veggie Beanburgers ILLUSTRATED RIGHT

SERVE THESE IN BURGER BUNS WITH A SELECTION OF YOUR FAVOURITE RELISHES SUCH AS CORN PICKLE, JALAPENO CHILLIES, TOMATO CHUTNEY OR WITH A MIXED SALAD.

SERVES 4

400-g/14-oz can chickpeas
400-g/14-oz can kidney beans
1 red onion
1 carrot
1 courgette
2 Tbsp oil, plus extra for deep-
    frying
50 g/2 oz finely chopped
    hazelnuts
1 Tbsp chopped fresh coriander
Salt and pepper
2 eggs
Flour, to dust
75 g/3 oz polenta or yellow
    cornmeal

1 Drain and rinse the chickpeas and kidney beans. Place the chickpeas in a food processor and grind to a meal. Mash or finely chop the kidney beans.

2 Peel and finely chop the onion and grate the carrot and courgette. Heat 2 tablespoons of oil in a small pan and fry the onion until soft but not browned.

3 Tip the onion into a bowl and stir in the chickpea meal, mashed kidney beans, grated carrot, courgette, chopped hazelnuts, coriander and seasoning. Beat 1 egg and stir in to bind the ingredients together.

4 Shape the mixture into 8 burgers and dust with flour. Beat the second egg, brush it over the burgers and coat them in the polenta. Chill for 2 hours to firm them up and allow the flavours to develop.

5 Heat about 2.5cm/1 in oil in a large frying pan to 180°C/350°F and fry the burgers in two batches for about 5 minutes or until golden brown, turning them over once. Serve hot with salad and relishes.

Fried Herb Garnishes

THESE CAN BE USED TO GARNISH ALL SORTS OF DISHES AND WILL TURN A SIMPLE RECIPE INTO
SOMETHING A BIT SPECIAL FOR A DINNER PARTY.

Basil or sage leaves
Sprigs of curly parsley
Oil for deep-frying

1 Choose large, unblemished basil or sage leaves and tight
sprigs of parsley with fairly long stalks. Rinse and blot with
kitchen paper until completely dry.

2 Heat 2.5 cm/1 in oil for frying in a deep pan to
180°C/350°F. Drop in the basil or sage leaves a few at a
time and fry for about 5 seconds until they darken, become
translucent and the edges begin to curl. Drain immediately.

3 The parsley can be fried in the same way, either as individual
sprigs or by tying several together with thin string and
lowering the bunch into the oil.

4 Garnish your chosen dish by scattering a few basil or sage
leaves over the top. The parsley can be placed in a bunch on
the side of the plate or crumbled over the dish.

Vegetable Tempura with a Vinegar Dipping Sauce

ALTHOUGH NOW ONE OF JAPAN'S MOST POPULAR DISHES, TEMPURA ONLY BECAME PART OF THE NATIONAL CUISINE WHEN SIXTEENTH CENTURY PORTUGUESE SETTLERS INTRODUCED LOCAL COOKS TO DEEP-FRYING. COOK THE VEGETABLES JUST BEFORE SERVING SO THEY ARE LIGHT AND CRISP.

SERVES 4

Dipping sauce:
6 Tbsp soy sauce
2 Tbsp rice vinegar
1 tsp fresh ginger purée

Tempura:
900 g/2 lb mixed vegetables,
    e.g., courgettes, broccoli
    florets, peppers, cauliflower
    florets, carrots, mushrooms
Oil for deep-frying
1 quantity of Tempura Batter
    (see page 14)

1 To make the dipping sauce, mix the ingredients together and pour into a serving dish.

2 For the tempura, prepare the vegetables as necessary, cutting into sticks or bite-size pieces. For firmer vegetables, such as carrots, broccoli and cauliflower, blanch the prepared pieces in a pan of boiling water for 2 to 3 minutes or until almost tender.

3 Heat oil for deep-frying to 190°C/375°F. Using chopsticks or tongs, dip the vegetable pieces in the batter one at a time and drop into the oil, frying 6 to 8 pieces at a time.

4 Fry for 2 to 4 minutes until the batter is golden, then remove the vegetables from the oil and drain. Serve at once with the dipping sauce.

Thai Sweetcorn Cakes with Peanut Sauce

IF SERVING THE PEANUT SAUCE COLD, REMEMBER IT WILL THICKEN UP ON STANDING SO YOU WILL NEED TO STIR IN A FEW TABLESPOONS OF WARM WATER TO THIN IT DOWN TO THE RIGHT CONSISTENCY.

SERVES 4-6

8 mangetout
100 g/4 oz sweetcorn kernels
    with peppers
1 Tbsp Thai green curry paste
1 Tbsp fish sauce
1 tsp brown sugar
1 Tbsp chopped fresh coriander
75 g/3 oz plain flour
1 egg, beaten
Oil for deep-frying

Peanut sauce:

1 small onion
1 garlic clove
1 small red chilli
1 Tbsp oil
4 Tbsp crunchy peanut butter
2 tsp brown sugar
1 tsp fish sauce
100 ml/¼ pt coconut milk

To garnish:

Red chilli, finely chopped
Spring onions, shredded
Coriander sprigs
Sweetcorn kernels

1 Finely chop the mangetout. In a bowl, mix together the sweetcorn, curry paste, fish sauce, brown sugar, coriander and mangetout. Stir in the flour until the ingredients are coated and then the egg to bind them together.

2 To make the sauce, peel and finely chop the onion, skin and crush the garlic, deseed and finely chop the chilli. Heat the oil in a saucepan and fry the onion until softened. Add the garlic and chilli and cook for 1 minute, then stir in the peanut butter, brown sugar, fish sauce and coconut milk. Heat gently, stirring frequently so the ingredients are evenly combined.

3 Heat oil for deep-frying to 180°C/350°F. Drop tablespoons of the sweetcorn mixture into the hot oil and fry for 3 to 4 minutes until golden brown. Drain and serve hot with the garnishes scattered over. Spoon a little warm peanut sauce on to each serving plate or serve the sauce cold as a dip, letting it down with warm water if it has become too thick.

Mushroom Spring Rolls

YOU CAN USE DRIED CHINESE MUSHROOMS OR ITALIAN PORCINI TO MAKE THESE CRISP ORIENTAL ROLLS. SOAK THE MUSHROOMS IN WATER FOR 30 MINUTES TO PLUMP THEM UP AND DRAIN WELL BEFORE ADDING TO THE FILLING. THE SOAKING WATER CAN BE KEPT AND ADDED TO SAUCES AND GRAVIES BUT STRAIN IT THROUGH A FINE SIEVE FIRST TO REMOVE ANY TINY PIECES OF GRIT FROM THE MUSHROOMS.

MAKES 12

15 g/½ oz dried mushrooms

350 g/12 oz brown cap mushrooms

½ red pepper

4 spring onions

225 g/8 oz cooked ham

2 Tbsp oil, plus extra for deep-frying

100 g/4 oz bean sprouts

1 tsp fresh ginger purée

1 Tbsp rice vinegar

2 Tbsp dark soy sauce

1 tsp sesame oil

1 Tbsp cornflour

12 spring roll wrappers

1 Place the dried mushrooms in a bowl, pour over boiling water to cover and set aside to soak for 30 minutes. Drain the mushrooms and chop any large pieces.

2 Finely chop the brown cap mushrooms, deseed and finely chop the red pepper, chop the spring onions and finely chop the ham.

3 Heat 2 tablespoons of oil in a frying pan, add the brown cap mushrooms, pepper and spring onions and fry for 5 minutes. Stir in the dried mushrooms, ham, beansprouts, ginger purée, rice vinegar, soy sauce and sesame oil and cook for 2 minutes. Set aside to cool.

4 In a small bowl, mix the cornflour with 4 tablespoons cold water until smooth. Divide the mushroom filling between the spring roll wrappers, brush the edges of the wrappers with the cornflour mix and roll up around the filling, tucking in the sides and pressing the edges together to seal.

5 Heat oil for deep-frying to 180°C/350°F and deep-fry the rolls for 4 to 5 minutes until golden brown. Drain and serve with a small bowl of dark soy sauce for dipping.

6 | just potatoes

The world's favourite snack has to be the ubiquitous chip. Thin
and stringy, short and fat, matchstick cut or traditional French
fries, a bag of chips must satisfy more hungry appetites than any
other food. Few people would argue that the humble potato is just
made for deep-frying and whichever way you do it the results are
equally delicious.

English Chip-shop Chips ILLUSTRATED ABOVE

THE TRADITIONAL ACCOMPANIMENT TO THAT GREAT BRITISH FAVOURITE, BATTERED FISH. THE CHIPS SHOULD BE SERVED IN NEWSPAPER ALONGSIDE THE FISH, LIBERALLY SPRINKLED WITH SALT AND MALT VINEGAR.

SERVES 4

900 g/2 lb floury potatoes
Oil for deep-frying
Salt
Malt vinegar

1 Peel and cut the potatoes into roughly 1 x 6 cm/½ x 2½-in batons. Rinse, drain and pat dry with kitchen paper.

2 Heat oil for deep-frying to 160°C/325°F, place half the chips in a frying basket and lower carefully into the hot oil. Fry for 5 minutes until the chips are soft but still pale-coloured. Drain and blanch the remaining chips in the same way.

3 When ready to serve, reheat the oil to 190°C/375°F. Return all the chips to the basket and fry for 3 to 4 minutes until crisp and golden, shaking the basket occasionally.

4 Drain, sprinkle with salt and malt vinegar and serve at once.

Buffalo Fries ILLUSTRATED LEFT

MAKE AS FOR ENGLISH CHIP-SHOP CHIPS BUT SCRUB THE POTATOES WELL AND LEAVE THE PEEL ON.

French Fries

THE ULTIMATE COMFORT FOOD! SERVE WITH BURGERS, SAUSAGES AND STEAKS, WITH MUSTARD OR KETCHUP OR, BEST OF ALL, ON THEIR OWN—CRISP, GOLDEN AND PIPING HOT.

SERVES 4

900 g/2 lb large floury potatoes
Oil for deep-frying
Salt

1 Peel and cut the potatoes into roughly ½ x 6-cm/¼ x 2½-inch batons. Rinse, drain, and pat dry with kitchen paper.

2 Heat oil for deep-frying to 160°C/325°F, place half the fries in a frying basket, and lower carefully into the hot oil. Fry for 5 minutes until the fries are soft but still pale-coloured. Drain and blanch the remaining fries in the same way.

3 When ready to serve, reheat the oil to 190°C/375°F. Return all the fries to the basket and fry for 2 minutes until crisp and golden, shaking the basket occasionally.

4 Drain, sprinkle with salt and serve at once.

TIPS FOR PERFECT CHIPS:

- When deep-frying potatoes, including chips, choose floury potatoes such as Maris Peer, King Edward, Pentland Dell and Maris Piper.

- Rinse the potatoes after you have cut them into chips or soak in a bowl of cold water to remove excess starch – this stops the chips sticking together in the frying basket.

- Prepare the chips ahead and soak in a bowl of salted water so they are crisper when cooked. Drain and pat dry thoroughly before frying.

- If you don't have a cooking thermometer, drop a chip into the hot oil and if it sinks and doesn't move the oil is not hot enough. The oil is ready when the chip floats and the oil bubbles around it.

Straw Potato Chips

CUT THE POTATOES INTO FINE JULIENNE STRIPS USING A SHARP KNIFE OR SAVE TIME BY PUSHING THEM THROUGH THE SHREDDING ATTACHMENT OF A FOOD PROCESSOR.

SERVES 4

450 g/1 lb floury potatoes
Oil for deep-frying
Salt

1 Peel and cut the potatoes into fine julienne strips. Wash, drain and dry thoroughly.

2 Heat oil for deep-frying to 190°C/375°F and fry the chips in small batches for 2 to 3 minutes until golden brown and crisp, shaking the basket or turning them over from time to time.

3 Drain, sprinkle with salt and serve with grilled meat or fish.

Matchstick Fries ILLUSTRATED BELOW

KNOWN AS 'POMMES ALLUMETTES' (MATCHSTICK POTATOES) IN FRANCE. CUT THE POTATOES INTO SLIGHTLY LARGER STRIPS THAN FOR THE STRAW POTATO CHIPS – 5 MM X 6 CM/¼ X 2½ IN – AND DEEP-FRY IN THE SAME WAY FOR 5 MINUTES OR UNTIL GOLDEN BROWN.

Game Chips ILLUSTRATED ABOVE

SERVE AS AN ACCOMPANIMENT TO ROAST PHEASANT AND OTHER GAME BIRDS OR TO NIBBLE WITH PRE-DINNER DRINKS.

SERVES 4

450 g/1 lb medium-sized floury
  potatoes
Oil for deep-frying
Salt

1 Peel the potatoes (or leave unpeeled, as preferred) and cut crossways into wafer thin slices. Immediately place in a bowl of cold water and leave to soak for 15 minutes to remove excess starch. Drain and dry thoroughly.

2 Heat oil for deep-frying to 190 °C/375 °F and fry the potato slices in small quantities for 2 minutes until crisp and golden brown, shaking the basket occasionally or turning the slices over.

3 Drain, sprinkle with salt and serve.

Lattice Chips ILLUSTRATED LEFT

MAKE AS FOR GAME CHIPS BUT CUT THE POTATO SLICES WITH A FLUTED VEGETABLE SLICER TO GIVE A HONEYCOMB EFFECT.

Skins with Guacamole Dip

WHEN SCOOPING OUT THE POTATO FLESH, LEAVE A 5-MM/¼-IN LAYER OF POTATO AROUND THE EDGE SO THE SKINS DON'T COLLAPSE AND TAKE CARE NOT TO SPLIT THE SKIN WITH THE SPOON.

SERVES 4

Guacamole dip:

2 medium tomatoes
½ small onion
1 to 2 green or red chillies
1 Tbsp fresh lime juice
Salt and pepper
2 ripe avocados
1 Tbsp chopped fresh parsley or
    coriander

Skin:

4 large baking potatoes
Oil for deep-frying

1 For the guacamole, finely chop the tomatoes, peel and finely chop or grate the onion and deseed and finely chop the chillies. Mix the tomatoes, onion, chillies and lime juice in a bowl and season with salt and pepper. Cover and set aside for 1 to 2 hours to allow the flavours to develop. Prepare the avocados for the dip no more than 30 minutes before serving or they will start to turn brown.

2 Score the potatoes around the centre with the point of a sharp knife. Bake in a preheated 200°C/400°F oven for 50 minutes to 1 hour or microwave for 20 minutes on full power until the potatoes are tender when pierced with a skewer.

3 Leave the potatoes until cool enough to handle, cut them in half and scoop out the flesh with a spoon. Cut the skins into fat wedges with a sharp knife.

4 Halve the avocados, remove the stones and scoop the flesh into a bowl, discarding the skins. Coarsely mash with a fork and then mix into the tomato mixture. Top with fresh parsley or coriander.

5 Heat oil for deep-frying to 190°C/375°F and fry the potato wedges for about 5 minutes until golden brown and crisp. Drain and serve with the guacamole.

Bubble and Squeak Cakes ILLUSTRATED LEFT

CHOOSE SAVOY CABBAGE OR ANOTHER VARIETY WITH DEEP GREEN LEAVES TO GIVE A GOOD COLOUR CONTRAST. SERVE THE CAKES ON THEIR OWN WITH BROWN SAUCE OR KETCHUP OR AS AN ACCOMPANIMENT.

SERVES 4

450 g/1 lb floury potatoes
1 medium carrot
100 g/4 oz dark green cabbage
    leaves, coarse stalks
    removed
4 spring onions
2 streaky bacon rashers
1 Tbsp oil, plus extra for deep-
    frying
4 Tbsp hot milk
Salt, pepper and nutmeg
Flour, to dust
1 egg, beaten
8 Tbsp dry breadcrumbs

1 Peel the potatoes, cut into chunks and cook in a pan of boiling water until tender.

2 Peel and grate the carrot, finely shred the cabbage leaves, finely chop the spring onions and chop the bacon rashers.

3 Heat 1 tablespoon of oil in a pan, add the bacon and cook until lightly browned. Add the carrot, cabbage and spring onions, cover the pan and cook over a gentle heat for 3 to 4 minutes or until the cabbage is tender.

4 Drain the potatoes and mash with the hot milk. Stir in the bacon and cabbage mixture and season with salt, pepper and a pinch of nutmeg. Leave to cool before shaping the mixture into 8 round, flat cakes. Dust the cakes with flour, brush with beaten egg and coat with the breadcrumbs. Chill for 1 hour.

5 Heat about 2.5 cm/1 in of oil in a large frying pan to 180°C/350°F and deep-fry the cakes for about 5 minutes until golden, turning over once. Drain and serve.

Almond Potato Bites

CRISP, NUTTY AND CRUNCHY, THESE COULD BE SERVED WITH ROAST CHICKEN, GRILLED PORK CHOPS OR BRAISED BEEF. CHOPPED HAZELNUTS OR PEANUTS CAN ALSO BE USED.

SERVES 4

675 g/1½ lb floury potatoes
50 g/2 oz butter
Salt and pepper
2 egg yolks
Flour, to dust
1 egg, beaten
75 g/3 oz finely chopped
    almonds
Oil for deep-frying

1 Peel the potatoes and cook in a pan of boiling water until tender. Drain and mash with the butter and seasoning.

2 Return the mash to the saucepan over a gentle heat, add the egg yolks and stir until the mixture leaves the bottom of the pan clean. Leave to cool.

3 Roll into golf ball-size balls and dust with flour. Brush with beaten egg and coat in the chopped almonds. Chill for 1 hour.

4 Heat oil for deep-frying to 180°C/350°F and fry in batches for 4 to 5 minutes until golden brown. Drain and serve.

Spiced New Potatoes

CHOOSE SMALL, EVEN-SIZED NEW POTATOES AND LEAVE THEIR SKINS ON. STEAM OR COOK IN A
PAN OF BOILING WATER UNTIL TENDER BEFORE COATING IN THE SPICE MIXTURE.

SERVES 4

1 egg white
½ tsp hot chilli powder
1 tsp ground coriander
½ tsp turmeric
50 g/2 oz flour
50 ml/2 fl oz water
Salt and pepper
75 g/3 oz dry breadcrumbs
1 tsp dried mint
700 g/1½ lb small new potatoes,
    cooked
Oil for deep-frying

Curried mayonnaise:
8 Tbsp mayonnaise
2 tsp curry paste

1 In a bowl, whisk the egg white until frothy, then whisk in
the chilli powder, coriander, turmeric, 50 g/2 oz flour,
water, salt and pepper.

2 Mix the breadcrumbs and oregano together. Dip in the spicy
batter and coat with the crumb mixture.

3 Heat oil for deep-frying to 190°C/375°F and deep-fry the
potatoes for 3 to 4 minutes until crisp and golden brown.
Drain and add a garnish of mint sprigs.

4 Stir the mayonnaise and curry paste together and serve with
the hot potatoes.

Potato and Parsnip Rolls

A HANDY WAY TO USE UP LEFT-OVER BOILED POTATOES AND PARSNIPS, THE ROLLS CAN BE MADE AHEAD OF TIME AND FROZEN UNTIL NEEDED.

SERVES 4

350 g/12 oz floury potatoes
250 g/9 oz parsnips
50 g/2 oz butter
2 egg yolks
50 g/2 oz grated Cheddar
    cheese
1 tsp fresh thyme leaves
1 Tbsp chopped fresh parsley
Salt and paprika
Flour, to dust
1 egg, beaten
75 g/3 oz dry breadcrumbs
Oil for deep-frying

1   Peel the potatoes and parsnips and cut into even-size pieces. Cook in a pan of boiling water until tender, drain and mash with the butter.

2   Return the mash to the saucepan over a gentle heat, stir in the egg yolks and continue stirring until the mash leaves the bottom of the saucepan clean. Remove from the heat and stir in the thyme, parsley, salt and paprika to taste. Leave to cool.

3   Mould the potato mixture into cork shapes, dust with flour, brush with beaten egg and coat in the breadcrumbs. Chill for 1 hour.

4   Heat oil for deep-frying to 180°C/350°F and deep-fry the rolls for 4 to 5 minutes until golden brown. Drain and serve.

Souffle Potatoes

AS WITH CHIPS, THESE LIGHT POTATO PUFFS NEED TO BE BLANCHED FIRST AND THEN RE-FRIED AT A HIGHER TEMPERATURE TO MAKE THEM GOLDEN AND CRISP.

SERVES 4

450 g/1 lb floury potatoes
Oil for deep-frying
Salt

1   Peel the potatoes and cut into 3-mm/⅛-in thick slices. Pat the slices dry with kitchen paper but don't soak them in cold water or rinse them. The starch will help them puff up.

2   Heat oil for deep-frying to 150°C/300°F and fry the slices in small batches because the starch will make them stick together. Fry each batch for 1 to 2 minutes, shaking the frying basket gently, until the slices begin to swell.

3   Drain and set aside until ready to serve – the puffed slices will sink back down but this is normal.

4   Reheat oil to 190°C/375°F, put all the slices back in the frying basket and plunge into the hot oil. Fry for 1 to 2 minutes or until puffed and golden brown. Drain and serve sprinkled with salt.

Pommes Dauphine

POPULAR IN FRANCE, THESE LIGHT, FLUFFY POTATO CROQUETTES ARE A MIX OF MASH AND CHOUX PASTE (A DOUGH USED FOR MAKING PROFITEROLES). SERVE THEM AS AN ACCOMPANIMENT TO PLAINLY GRILLED CHICKEN OR PORK WITH A CREAMY RED PEPPER SAUCE.

SERVES 4

Red pepper sauce:
1 garlic clove
1 red pepper
1 Tbsp oil
1 tsp sweet chilli sauce
400-g/14-oz can chopped
   tomatoes
1 tsp sugar
100 ml/4 fl oz single cream
Snipped chives, to garnish

Potatoes:
450 g/1 lb floury potatoes
100 g/4 oz butter
Salt and pepper
150 ml/¼ pt water
100 g/4 oz plain flour
2 medium eggs, beaten
Oil for deep-frying

1 To make the sauce, peel and crush the garlic, deseed and chop the pepper.

2 Heat the oil in a pan and fry the garlic and pepper until softened. Add the chilli sauce, tomatoes and sugar, cover the pan and simmer for 30 minutes. Liquidise the sauce and stir in the cream.

3 For the potatoes, peel, cut into chunks and cook in a pan of boiling water until tender. Drain, mash with half the butter and season with salt and pepper.

4 Cut up the rest of the butter into small pieces and place in a pan with the water. Heat until the butter melts, then bring to a fast boil. Remove the pan from the heat, tip in all the flour and beat with a wooden spoon until the mixture forms a smooth ball that leaves the sides of the pan.

5 Cool slightly, then beat in the eggs a little at a time. Stir this mixture into the potato mash and leave to cool.

6 Heat oil for deep-frying to 170°C/325°F. Using two large spoons, scoop the mixture into egg-shaped croquettes and drop into the hot oil. Fry for 4 to 5 minutes until golden brown. Drain and serve with the warmed sauce and snipped chives sprinkled over.

Sweet Potato Fritters with Tomato Salsa

ADD EXTRA CHILLI TO THE SALSA IF YOU LIKE THINGS HOT. THE FRITTERS CAN ALSO BE SERVED AS AN ACCOMPANIMENT TO GRILLED MEATS AND FISH.

SERVES 4 TO 6

Fritters:
700 g/1½ lb sweet potatoes
1 onion
2 garlic cloves
½ red pepper
2 Tbsp oil, plus extra for deep-frying
1 Tbsp chopped fresh parsley
Flour, to dust
1 egg, beaten
50 g/2 oz fresh wholemeal breadcrumbs

Salsa:
350 g/12 oz tomatoes
2 sticks of celery
3 spring onions
1 red chilli
1 Tbsp chopped fresh mint
2 Tbsp white wine vinegar

1 To make the fritters, peel the sweet potatoes, boil and mash. Peel and finely chop the onion, peel and crush the garlic, deseed and finely chop the pepper.

2 Heat 2 tablespoons of oil in a frying pan and cook the onion until soft. Add the garlic and pepper and fry for 2 to 3 minutes. Stir in the parsley, mix into the sweet potato mash and leave to cool.

3 Shape the mixture into small balls. Dust with flour, coat in the beaten egg and roll in the breadcrumbs. Chill for 1 hour to firm up.

4 To make the salsa, peel, deseed and chop the tomatoes, finely chop the celery, trim and slice the spring onions, deseed and finely chop the chilli. Mix the tomatoes, celery, onions and chilli with the mint and vinegar and chill until ready to serve.

5 Heat oil for deep-frying to 190°C/375°F and fry the fritters in batches for 2 to 3 minutes until golden brown. Drain and serve hot with the salsa.

7 | doughnuts & other sweet treats

Doughnuts are the favourite childhood treat that every grownup loves as well. The perfect doughnut should be light and spongy with a crisp white sugar coating and if they're good one will never be enough. America is the doughnut capital of the world but variations on the traditional jam-filled or iced ring doughnut pop up in many other countries. The Spaniards dip finger-shaped churros into mugs of rich hot chocolate, the Greeks enjoy loukomathes scooped into paper cones and drenched with honey. If you have a sweet tooth, you'll find plenty to tempt you in this chapter.

Cannoli

THESE CRISP PASTRY TUBES FILLED WITH RICOTTA CHEESE AND GLACÉ FRUITS ARE A SICILIAN SPECIALITY WHERE THEY TAKE PRIDE OF PLACE IN THE LOCAL CAKE SHOPS. CANNOLI MOULDS CAN BE BOUGHT FROM KITCHENWARE STORES OR ASK AT YOUR LOCAL HARDWARE SHOP FOR FOUR PIECES OF STAINLESS STEEL TUBING, AROUND 15 CM/6 IN LONG AND 2 CM/3/4 IN IN DIAMETER. IN SICILY, COOKS WOULD PROBABLY USE OLIVE OIL TO FRY THE PASTRY BUT OTHER LESS FLAVOURED OILS SUCH AS GROUNDNUT OR VEGETABLE WORK EQUALLY WELL.

MAKES 16

Pastry:
175 g/6 oz plain flour
¼ tsp salt
50 g/2 oz butter
40 g/1½ oz caster sugar
1 egg, beaten
2 to 3 Tbsp white wine or dry
    Marsala, to mix
1 egg white, lightly beaten
Oil for deep-frying

Filling:
50 g/2 oz dark chocolate
350 g/12 oz ricotta or curd
    cheese
50 g/2 oz icing sugar
Finely grated zest of 1 orange
50 g/2 oz chopped glacé fruits,
    e.g., candied citrus peel
Extra icing sugar, to dust

1 To make the pastry, sift the flour and salt into a bowl and rub in the butter until like fine breadcrumbs. Stir in the sugar, then mix in the egg and enough wine or Marsala to make a soft but not sticky dough. Knead until smooth and roll out thinly on a floured surface.

2 Cut the pastry into 16 squares, roughly 7.5 cm/3 in in size. Dust four metal cannoli tubes with flour and wrap a pastry square loosely around each on the diagonal, dampening the edges with lightly beaten egg white and pressing them together to seal.

3 Heat oil for deep-frying to 180°C/350°F and deep fry for 3 to 4 minutes or until the pastry is golden and crisp. Drain and when cool enough to handle, rotate the metal tubes gently so you can pull them out of the pastry. Cook three more batches of pastry tubes in the same way.

4 To make the filling, very finely chop or grate the chocolate and mix with the cheese, icing sugar, orange zest and glacé fruits. When the pastry tubes are cold, pipe or spoon the filling into them. Dust with icing sugar and eat on the day they are made.

Basic Doughnut Dough

IT IS ESPECIALLY IMPORTANT TO HEAT THE OIL TO THE CORRECT TEMPERATURE WHEN FRYING DOUGHNUTS. TOO COOL AND THEY WILL ABSORB TOO MUCH OIL, BECOMING HEAVY AND FATTY INSTEAD OF LIGHT AND CRISP, TOO HOT AND THE OUTSIDE OF THE DOUGHNUTS WILL BURN WHILE THE CENTRES STAY STICKY AND UNDER-DONE. DOUGHNUTS ARE BEST EATEN ON THE DAY THEY ARE MADE.

450 g/1 lb self-raising flour
1 Tbsp baking powder
75 g/3 oz caster sugar
2 eggs
225 ml/8 fl oz milk
50 g/2 oz butter, melted and
   cooled

1 Sift the flour and baking powder into a mixing bowl and stir in the caster sugar.

2 Beat together the eggs, milk and melted butter, add to the dry ingredients and mix to a soft dough. Cover the bowl and chill for 1 hour to firm up the dough.

Plain Sugar-dusted Doughnuts

ADD A FESTIVE TOUCH BY MIXING THE DUSTING SUGAR WITH A LITTLE POWDERED FOOD COLOURING. PUT THE SUGAR AND COLOURING INTO A SMALL PLASTIC BAG, TWIST THE TOP TO SEAL AND SHAKE WELL.

MAKES 12

1 quantity of Basic Doughnut
   Dough (see above)
Oil for deep-frying
Caster sugar, to dust

1 Make up the dough as directed. Divide it into 12 pieces and roll into balls.

2 Heat oil for deep-frying to 180°C/350°F and fry the doughnuts in batches for about 8 to 10 minutes or until puffed and golden brown.

3 Drain, sprinkle generously with caster sugar and leave to cool before serving.

Ring Doughnuts with Vanilla and Chocolate Frosting

RATHER THAN WASTING THE THE CUT-OUT CENTRES, THEY CAN BE TURNED INTO MINI DOUGHNUT BITES WITH MAPLE SYRUP AND STRAWBERRIES.

MAKES ABOUT 16

1 quantity of Basic Doughnut Dough (see page 134)
½ tsp ground cinnamon
Oil for deep-frying
Caster sugar, to dust

Frosting:
350 g/12 oz icing sugar
4 to 5 Tbsp warm water
75 g/3 oz plain chocolate, melted
Few drops of vanilla essence
Chocolate vermicelli
Hundreds and thousands

1 Make up the dough, adding the cinnamon to the flour and baking powder.

2 Roll out the dough on a floured surface about 1-cm/½-in thick. Flour a 7.5-cm/3-in plain pastry cutter and stamp out rounds. Cut holes out of the centre of each round with a floured 2.5-cm/1-in cutter.

3 Heat 4 cm/1½ in oil for frying in a wide heavy pan to 180°C/350°F. Fry the doughnuts two or three at a time for about 5 minutes until golden, turning over once or twice. Drain, sprinkle with a little caster sugar and leave to cool.

4 Sift the icing sugar into a bowl and stir in enough warm water to make a smooth icing. Spoon half the icing into another bowl and add the vanilla essence to one bowl and the melted chocolate to the other.

5 Spread the top of half the doughnuts with the vanilla icing and the rest with the chocolate icing. Sprinkle with chocolate vermicelli and hundreds and thousands. Leave to set.

Gulab Jamun

A STYLISH INDIAN DESSERT THAT WOULD MAKE A FITTING FINALE TO A DINNER PARTY OF CURRIED OR SPICED DISHES. LEAVE THE CRISP-FRIED DOUGH BALLS TO COOL IN THE ROSEWATER SYRUP SO THEY BECOME SOFT AND SPONGY AND SERVE IN INDIVIDUAL BOWLS WITH A FEW ROSE PETALS FOR DECORATION. DO NOT USE PETALS FROM A ROSE BOUGHT AT A FLORIST'S SHOP BECAUSE THEY ARE LIKELY TO HAVE BEEN SPRAYED WITH CHEMICALS.

SERVES 4

100 g/4 oz plain flour
½ tsp baking powder
6 Tbsp full-fat milk powder
50 g/2 oz butter
About 4 Tbsp milk
Oil for deep-frying

Syrup:
225 g/8 oz sugar
4 Tbsp water
1 Tbsp rose water

To serve:
Rose petals

1 Sift the flour, baking powder and milk powder into a bowl. Rub in the butter until like breadcrumbs and add enough milk to mix to an elastic dough.

2 Divide the dough into 16 pieces and roll into balls.

3 Heat oil for deep-frying to 180°C/350°F and fry the balls in batches for 4 to 5 minutes or until golden brown. Drain the balls as they cook and then transfer in a large heatproof bowl.

4 To make the syrup, heat the sugar and water in a pan until the sugar dissolves. Bring to the boil and simmer for 1 minute. Stir in the rose water and pour the hot syrup over the dough balls. Leave to cool.

5 To serve, wash and dry the rose petals. Divide the dough balls and syrup between individual serving dishes and float a few rose petals on each.

Traditional Jam Doughnuts

SEAL THE JAM TIGHTLY INSIDE THE DOUGH OR IT WILL LEAK OUT DURING FRYING. YOU CAN USE YOUR FAVOURITE JAM TO FILL THE DOUGHNUTS BUT THOSE WITH A STRONG FRUIT FLAVOUR SUCH AS RASPBERRY, STRAWBERRY, APRICOT OR BLACKBERRY WORK THE BEST.

MAKES 12

1 quantity of Basic Doughnut Dough (see page 134)
About 2 Tbsp jam
Oil for deep-frying
Caster sugar, to dust

1 Make up the dough. Roll out about 1-cm/½-in thick and cut out 6-cm/2½-in rounds using a plain cutter, gathering up and re-rolling the trimmings until you have 24 rounds.

2 Spoon a little jam into the centre of 12 of the rounds. Brush the edges with water and press the remaining rounds on top, pressing and pinching the edges together to make a tight seal.

3 Heat oil for deep-frying to 180°C/350°F and fry the doughnuts in batches for about 10 minutes until golden brown, turning them over occasionally so they colour evenly. Drain, sprinkle with caster sugar and leave to cool.

Apple Doughnut Parcels

SERVE THESE JUST WARM AS A DELICIOUS DESSERT WITH PLENTY OF WHIPPED CREAM OR
VANILLA ICE CREAM.

MAKES 12

2 medium-sized tart apples

2 Tbsp golden raisins

2 Tbsp orange juice

Sugar, to taste

1 quantity of Basic Doughnut
   Dough (see page 134)

1 egg white, lightly beaten

Oil for deep-frying

Caster sugar and ground
   cinnamon, to dust

1 Peel, core and chop the apples. Place in a non-stick pan with the golden raisins and orange juice, cover and simmer gently until the apples are soft but not falling apart. Add sugar to taste and leave to cool.

2 Make up the dough and roll out about 1-cm/½-in thick. Dust a sharp knife with flour and cut out 7.5-cm/3-in squares of dough, gathering up and re-rolling the trimmings as necessary until you have 12 squares.

3 Drain any excess liquid from the apple mixture and spoon a little on one side of each dough square. Brush the edges of the squares with egg white and fold one corner over the filling to meet the opposite corner and make a triangular-shaped parcel, pinching the edges together to seal.

4 Heat oil for deep-frying to 180°C/350°F and fry the doughnut parcels in batches for about 5 minutes, turning them over occasionally, until golden brown. Drain and dust with a mix of caster sugar and ground cinnamon – add about ½ tsp cinnamon to 3 tablespoons sugar.

Loukoumathes

THESE SMALL STICKY DOUGHNUTS ARE POPULAR IN GREECE WHERE THEY ARE EATEN AS AN ACCOMPANIMENT TO THE THICK, SEMI-SWEET GREEK COFFEE CALLED METRIO. AFTER FRYING, DRIZZLE THE DOUGHNUTS WITH SYRUP AND DUST WITH CINNAMON BEFORE SERVING.

SERVES 6

350 g/12 oz plain flour
1 tsp sugar
Pinch of salt
7-g/¼-oz sachet of easy-blend
    dried yeast
225 ml/8 fl oz lukewarm water
Oil for deep-frying

Syrup:
100 ml/4 fl oz runny honey
2 Tbsp lemon juice

To serve:
Ground cinnamon

1 Sift the flour into a bowl and stir in the sugar, salt and yeast. Make a well in the centre, pour in the water and mix to a soft dough. Knead on a floured surface until smooth. Transfer to a lightly oiled plastic bag, seal the top and leave in a warm place until the dough has doubled in size.

2 Split open the bag and, with your fingers, pinch off small walnut-sized pieces of dough on to a plate.

3 Heat oil for deep-frying to 180°C/350°F and cook the dough balls in batches for about 5 to 6 minutes until deep golden brown, turning them over as they cook so they brown evenly. Drain.

4 For the syrup, warm the honey and lemon juice in a pan and drizzle over the hot doughnuts. Dust with ground cinnamon and serve warm.

Caramelised Walnuts

SERVE THESE WITH AFTER-DINNER COFFEE AS A DELICIOUS ALTERNATIVE TO CHOCOLATES OR PETITS FOURS. BLANCHING THE WALNUTS BEFORE FRYING REMOVES ANY BITTER FLAVOUR THEY MIGHT HAVE.

SERVES 6

250 g/9 oz walnut halves
100 g/3 oz cup clear honey
1 Tbsp lemon juice
175 g/6 oz caster sugar
Oil for deep-frying
4 Tbsp sesame seeds

1 Simmer the walnut halves in a pan of boiling water for 2 minutes. Drain and dry with kitchen paper.

2 In a bowl, mix together the honey and lemon juice, add the walnuts and stir until coated. Set aside for 2 to 3 hours, stirring occasionally.

3 Spread out the caster sugar on a plate, drain the walnuts and coat them in the sugar.

4 Heat oil for deep-frying to 180°C/350°F. Fry the walnuts in two batches for about 2 minutes each until just golden – don't let the oil get too hot or the walnuts colour too much or they will taste burnt and bitter.

5 Drain the walnuts on a sheet of greaseproof paper (avoid using kitchen paper as they will stick) and sprinkle with the sesame seeds. Serve warm or cold.

Creamy Chocolate Filos

SERVE THESE HOT SO THAT WHEN YOU BREAK INTO THE CRISP FILO SHELL, THE CREAMY DARK
CHOCOLATE CENTRE OOZES OUT. SERVE THEM ON THEIR OWN OR WITH ICE CREAM.

MAKES 12

100 g/4 oz white almond paste
75 g/3 oz cream cheese
1 tsp finely grated lemon zest
1 tsp lemon juice
2 tsp plain flour
6 sheets of filo pastry,
    measuring 19 x 30 cm /
    7 x 12 in
12 small squares of dark
    chocolate
1 egg white, lightly beaten
Oil for deep-frying

1 Finely chop the almond paste and place in a bowl. Stir in the cream cheese, lemon zest, juice and flour until evenly combined. Chill the mixture for 1 hour.

2 Cut the filo sheets in half lengthways to give 12 long strips. Spoon a little of the almond mixture at the end of one strip and place a square of chocolate on top. Fold the corner of the pastry diagonally over the filling and continue folding up the strip to make a triangular parcel. Dab a little egg white on the top edges of the pastry and press them together to seal.

3 Repeat with the remaining filo strips and filling to make 12 parcels. Heat oil for deep-frying to 180°C/350°F and fry the parcels for 2 to 3 minutes until golden brown and crisp. Drain and serve warm.

Churros

IN SPAIN THESE SMALL, FINGER-SHAPED DOUGHNUTS ARE EATEN AS AN ACCOMPANIMENT TO
THICK, CREAMY HOT CHOCOLATE.

SERVES 4

175 g/6 oz plain flour
Pinch of salt
225 ml/8 fl oz water
1 egg, beaten
Oil for deep-frying
Caster sugar, to dust

1 Sift the flour and salt together on to a plate. Bring the water to a fast boil and tip in all the flour. Remove the pan from the heat and beat vigorously with a wooden spoon until the dough forms a ball and leaves the sides of the pan clean.

2 Gradually beat in the egg until the mixture is smooth, shiny and holds its shape.

3 Spoon the mixture into a piping bag fitted with a large star nozzle, pushing it in firmly so there are no air bubbles. Heat oil for deep-frying to 180°C/350°F and pipe 7.5 to 10-cm/ 3 to 4-in lengths into the oil, cutting off each length with a knife and letting it fall gently into the oil.

4 Fry the churros in batches until golden brown, for about 2 to 3 minutes. Drain, dredge with caster sugar and eat while still warm – if left to go cold they will become tough and chewy.

8 | fruity desserts

Deep-fried fruit is unbeatable if you want a truly satisfying

dessert. When it comes to rounding off a great Chinese

meal, top of everyone's list is sesame toffee fritters.

Filo pastry fries to a deliciously crisp shell and can be

wrapped around any number of fruit fillings. Tangy

sauces made with sharper-flavoured fruits such as

raspberries or blueberries make excellent accompaniments

to plain fritters or beignets. Flavour the fritters

with spices like cinnamon or

ginger and serve.

Tropical Fruit Salad with Gingered French Toast ILLUSTRATED LEFT

ANY COMBINATION OF TROPICAL FRUITS CAN BE USED, SUCH AS MANGO, PAPAYA, PINEAPPLE, BANANA, STAR FRUIT AND LYCHEES. SERVE WITH WHIPPED CREAM OR CRÈME FRAICHE.

SERVES 6

900 g/2 lb mixed tropical fruits
6 Tbsp fresh pineapple juice
2 Tbsp rum, optional

French toast:
3 eggs
100 ml/4 fl oz milk
2 Tbsp caster sugar
1 tsp ground ginger
6 large slices of thick-sliced
    white bread
Oil for deep-frying
Icing sugar, to dust

1 Prepare the fruit as necessary and cut into bite-sized pieces. Place in a bowl, spoon over the pineapple juice and rum (if using) and chill in the refrigerator until ready to serve.

2 To make the French toast, whisk together the eggs, milk, sugar and ginger in a shallow dish. Cut each bread slice into two or four triangles.

3 Heat oil for deep-frying to 180°C/350°F. Dip the bread in the egg mixture until well coated and fry in batches for 1 to 2 minutes until golden brown. Drain, dust with icing sugar and serve hot with the fruit salad.

Cherry Almond Filos

IF USING CANNED OR BOTTLED CHERRIES, DRAIN THEM THOROUGHLY AND PAT DRY WITH ABSORBENT KITCHEN PAPER SO EXCESS JUICE DOESN'T SEEP INTO THE PASTRY.

SERVES 6

75 g/3 oz cream cheese
90 g/3½ oz ground almonds
25 g/1 oz soft light brown sugar
225 g/8 oz pitted cherries
6 sheets of filo pastry, each 30 x
    19 cm/12 x 7 in
Oil for deep-frying
Icing sugar, to dredge

1 In a bowl, mix together the cream cheese, ground almonds and sugar. Roughly chop the cherries and stir in.

2 Place a sheet of filo on a board and spoon one-sixth of the mixture down the centre. Brush the pastry edges with oil and roll it around the filling, tucking in the sides to make a log shape. Repeat with the rest of the filo and filling to make six parcels.

3 Heat oil for deep-frying to 170°C/325°F and deep-fry the parcels in two batches for 3 to 4 minutes each until golden. Drain and dredge with icing sugar before serving warm with whipped cream or vanilla ice cream.

Chinese Toffee Fruit Fritters

WHEN MAKING THE TOFFEE, ENSURE THE SUGAR DISSOLVES COMPLETELY BEFORE YOU BRING IT
TO THE BOIL OR YOU WILL HAVE AN UNPLEASANTLY GRANULAR CARAMEL.

SERVES 4

100 g/4 oz plain flour, plus
    extra for dusting
2 tsp oil, plus extra for deep-
    frying
1 tart dessert apple
2 pineapple rings
1 medium banana
Sesame oil for greasing
Ice cubes
350 g/12 oz caster sugar
3 Tbsp mixed black and white
    sesame seeds

1 Sift the flour into a bowl, stir in about 150 ml/¼ pint cold water to make a smooth batter and then stir in 2 teaspoons vegetable oil. Leave to stand for 30 minutes.

2 Peel and core the apples and cut each one into eight wedges. Cut each pineapple ring into quarters, peel and cut the banana into 4 chunks.

3 Heat oil for deep-frying to 190°C/375°F. Dust the fruit with flour and drop about six pieces into the batter. Lift them out one at a time with a slotted spoon and carefully place in the oil – adding the fruit pieces one at a time prevents them sticking together as they fry.

4 Fry for 2 to 3 minutes until golden, remove and drain on kitchen paper. Fry the remaining fruit in the same way.

5 Grease a large plate with a little sesame oil and have ready a bowl filled with cold water and ice cubes.

6 To make the caramel, heat the caster sugar in a heavy-based pan with 175 ml/6 fl oz water until the sugar dissolves. Bring to the boil and boil until the syrup caramelises to a rich golden brown. Remove the pan from the heat and add the sesame seeds and fruit pieces, tossing until coated with the caramel.

7 Turn out at once on to the greased plate and, using two forks, dip the pieces one at a time into the iced water to set the toffee coating. Serve hot.

Apple Fritter Rings with Apricot Sauce

USE FIRM DESSERT APPLES RATHER THAN COOKING APPLES THAT WILL SOFTEN TOO MUCH WHEN THEY COOK.

SERVES 4

Apricot sauce:
175 g/6 oz no-soak dried apricots
450 ml/16 fl oz orange juice

Fritters:
3 dessert apples
Flour, to dust
Oil for deep-frying
1 quantity of Yeast Batter (see page 14)
1 tsp ground cinnamon
Pinch of ground nutmeg
2 tsp icing sugar

1 To make the sauce, simmer the apricots and orange juice in a covered pan for 10 minutes or until the apricots are soft. Purée in a liquidiser or food processor and dilute if necessary with extra juice.

2 To make the fritters, core the apples and peel if preferred. Cut the apples into 5-mm/¼-in rings and dust with flour.

3 Heat oil for deep-frying to 180°C/350°F. Stir the batter, dip the apple rings in it until coated and fry three or four at a time until crisp and golden brown. Drain and sprinkle with the cinnamon, nutmeg and icing sugar. Serve with the warm sauce.

Apple Funnel Cakes ILLUSTRATED LEFT

COOK THESE IN A DEEP FRYING PAN OR OTHER WIDE PAN, POURING THE BATTER CAREFULLY INTO THE HOT OIL IN A SLOW STEADY STREAM FROM A TEAPOT.

MAKES 6

150 g/5 oz plain flour
1 tsp baking powder
175 ml/6 fl oz unsweetened
    apple juice
1 egg, beaten
1 tsp ground ginger
Oil for deep-frying
3 Tbsp caster sugar

1 Sift the flour and baking powder into a bowl, make a well in the centre, and gradually whisk in the apple juice, beaten egg, and half the ginger to make a smooth batter. Leave to stand for 1 hour. Add more water if the batter is too thick.

2 Pour one-third of the batter into a teapot or similar vessel. Heat about 1 inch of oil in a large frying pan to 170 °C/ 325 °F and slowly pour batter into the oil in a tight spiral, approximately 15cm/6 in in diameter. Fry for 3 to 4 minutes until golden brown, turning the spiral over after 2 minutes. Drain and fry the rest of the batter to make six cakes.

3 Mix the remaining ginger with the caster sugar and toss the hot cakes in it. Serve warm with caramelised apple slices – melt 50 g/2 oz butter in a pan and sprinkle over 4 tablespoons caster sugar, stirring until it dissolves. Add the apple slices and cook until caramelised. Spoon over the apple cakes with the buttery juices in the pan.

Banana Fritters with Orange Cream

FRUIT FRITTERS, SIMILAR TO THESE MADE WITH MASHED BANANA, ARE POPULAR IN THE WEST INDIES WHERE BOTH BANANAS AND SWEET SPICES LIKE NUTMEG AND CINNAMON ARE PLENTIFUL.

SERVES 6

Cream:
225 ml/8 fl oz double cream
Finely grated zest of 1 orange

Fritters:
900 g/2 lb bananas (unpeeled)
2 eggs, beaten
½ tsp ground allspice
¼ tsp grated nutmeg
1 Tbsp light muscovado sugar
2 tsp baking powder
Oil for deep-frying
Caster sugar, to dust

1 To make the cream, whisk the double cream and orange zest together until standing in soft peaks. Spoon into a serving dish and chill until needed.

2 To make the fritters, peel and mash the bananas. Add the eggs, allspice, nutmeg, muscovado sugar and baking powder and beat to form a thick batter.

3 Heat 2.5 cm/1 in oil in a large frying pan and drop in small spoonfuls of the batter. Fry for 2 to 3 minutes until golden, turning over once.

4 Drain the fritters, dust liberally with caster sugar and serve warm with the cream.

Fruit Tempura with Raspberry Sauce

THE FRUIT NEEDS TO BE RIPE SO THE STONES CAN BE REMOVED EASILY BUT NOT TOO SOFT OR IT WILL BE DIFFICULT TO RE-SHAPE AROUND THE HAZELNUT FILLING.

SERVES 4

Raspberry Sauce:
450 g/1 lb raspberries
100 g/4 oz caster sugar

Tempura:
40 g/1½ oz shelled hazelnuts
1 Tbsp brown sugar
3 Tbsp cream cheese
6 red plums
6 apricots or yellow plums
Flour, to dust
1 quantity of Tempura Batter
(see page 14)
Oil for deep-frying
Flour, to dust
½ tsp finely shredded nutmeg

1 To make the sauce, simmer the raspberries and sugar together until the fruit is soft. Purée and, if you prefer a smooth sauce, push through a sieve to remove the seeds.

2 To make the tempura, finely chop the hazelnuts and mix with the sugar and cream cheese.

3 Halve the plums and apricots, remove the stones and then sandwich the halves back together with the hazelnut mixture.

4 Make up the batter and heat oil for deep-frying to 190°C/375°F. Dust the fruit with flour, dip in the batter and fry three or four at a time for about 3 minutes until golden and crisp.

5 Drain the tempura and serve with the warm sauce. Sprinkle over the nutmeg.

Cinnamon Puffs with Blueberry Sauce

OTHER FRUITS COULD BE USED TO MAKE THE SAUCE SUCH AS BLACKCURRANTS, RASPBERRIES OR APRICOTS. IF USING FRUIT THAT HAS BEEN CANNED OR BOTTLED IN SYRUP, OMIT THE SUGAR FROM THE RECIPE AND FOR LARGER FRUITS, PURÉE THE SAUCE IN A BLENDER BEFORE ADDING THE ARROWROOT.

SERVES 6

Sauce:
450 g/1 lb blueberries
100 ml/4 fl oz water
50 g/2 oz caster sugar
Juice of 1 orange
1 Tbsp arrowroot

Cinnamon puffs:
100 g/4 oz plain flour
1 tsp ground cinnamon
150 ml/¼ pt water
50 g/2 oz butter, cut into small pieces
2 medium eggs, beaten
Finely grated zest of ½ orange
1 Tbsp caster sugar
Oil for deep-frying

To finish:
Fine shreds of orange zest
Caster sugar, to dust

1 To make the sauce, simmer the blueberries, water, sugar and orange juice together in a covered pan for 15 minutes or until the blueberries are soft, mashing them occasionally with a spoon. Mix the arrowroot with 2 tablespoons cold water and set aside.

2 To make the puffs, sift the flour and cinnamon on to a sheet of greaseproof paper. Heat the water and butter in a pan until the butter melts. Bring to a fast boil, remove from the heat and tip in all the flour. Beat with a wooden spoon until the mixture forms a smooth ball that leaves the sides of the pan.

3 Cool for a few minutes, then beat in the eggs a little at a time with the orange zest and sugar.

4 Heat oil for deep-frying to 170°C/325°F. Drop teaspoonfuls of the mixture into the oil and fry in batches for 4 to 5 minutes until puffed and golden brown. Drain and keep warm in a low oven.

5 Stir the arrowroot and mix into the sauce. Reheat gently over a low heat until the sauce thickens, stirring occasionally.

6 Serve the warm puffs sprinkled with orange zest and dusted with caster sugar with the hot sauce spooned around.

Mango and Ice Cream Parcels

IT'S IMPORTANT TO WORK QUICKLY WHEN ASSEMBLING THE PARCELS SO THE ICE CREAM HAS NO TIME TO MELT. ALTHOUGH THEY NEED TO BE FRIED AND SERVED STRAIGHT AWAY, THE PARCELS CAN BE MADE AHEAD OF TIME AND KEPT IN THE FREEZER UNTIL 10 MINUTES BEFORE FRYING. ONCE COOKED THEY HAVE TO BE SERVED IMMEDIATELY – LIKE A SOUFFLE, DINERS MUST WAIT FOR THEM, NOT THE OTHER WAY ROUND!

SERVES 6

2 ripe mangos
6 sheets of filo pastry,
  measuring roughly
  19 x 30 cm/7 x 12 in
1 egg white, lightly beaten
6 scoops of vanilla ice cream
Oil for deep-frying
Icing sugar, to dust

1 Place a baking tray in the freezer.

2 Peel the mangos and cut the flesh away from the stone. Chop the flesh into small pieces.

3 Lay a sheet of filo lengthways on the worktop and spoon one-sixth of the mango flesh at one corner about 5 cm/2 in from the edge. Brush the pastry edges with egg white and place a scoop of ice cream on top of the mango.

4 Working quickly, fold the pastry corner over the mango and ice cream and roll up the pastry around the filling, tucking in the side flaps and sealing the edges. As soon as you have assembled the parcel, place it on the baking tray in the freezer.

5 Make five more parcels in the same way, transferring each one immediately to the freezer as soon as it is made.

6 Remove the parcels from the freezer 10 minutes before cooking. Heat oil for deep-frying to 190 °C/375 °F and fry the parcels two at a time for 2 minutes until golden brown, turning over halfway. Drain the first two parcels when they are cooked, dredge with icing sugar and serve these before you fry the next batch.

Index